DINOMANIA

Dinomania

Why We Love, Fear and Are Utterly Enchanted by Dinosaurs

Boria Sax

REAKTION BOOKS

To the little boy I used to be, in the hope that
he may yet grow up to be a dinosaur.

Published by
Reaktion Books Ltd
Unit 32, Waterside
44–48 Wharf Road
London N1 7UX, UK
www.reaktionbooks.co.uk

First published 2018

Printed and bound in China by 1010 Printing International Ltd

A catalogue record for this book is available from the British Library

ISBN 978 1 78914 004 0

Contents

Draco bipes apteros captus in
Agro Bononiensi.

Matthäus Merian, engraving of a dragon, 1718. Like many dragons of the
early modern period and earlier, this one shows a noteworthy resemblance
to a dinosaur, especially with its extended neck and tail.

CHAPTER I

Dragon Bones

In your secret heart of hearts you wanted brontosaurus,
tame of course, to come back in the world.
RAY BRADBURY, *Dinosaur Tales*

People have always known of dinosaurs, though they have called
them by many names. Old legends that place Western dragons
in caves or beneath the earth may have originated with fossils.
The plumed serpent, prominent in mythologies of Mexico and Latin
America, is often a creator of life. The Rainbow Serpent of Aboriginal
tales was present at the beginning of time, and helped prepare the
landscapes for human beings and other animals. The Asian dragon,
which combines features of many animals, symbolizes primordial
energy and is the bringer of rain. These figures resemble our reconstructions of dinosaurs in appearance, and accounts place them in
worlds that existed before humankind. The major reason for this similarity might be that human imagination works in much the same way
as evolution. Both constantly recycle familiar forms such as wings,
claws, crests, fangs and scales, which may repeatedly vanish and then
reappear through convergence. The figure of *Tyrannosaurus rex* suggests
a kangaroo, while pterosaurs resemble bats, but the similarities are
not due to common ancestry.

Children, who are just learning the basic expectations of their society, are in ways outside of culture. Their attraction to dinosaurs suggests that the giant creatures appeal to something innate, or at least very elemental, in the human psyche. One highly speculative explanation is that this is a genetic legacy, going back to the days when early humans faced gigantic, prehistoric lizards such as the megalania or perhaps even the days when our remote mammalian ancestors had to contend with dinosaurs themselves. A simpler explanation is that images of dinosaurs convey the excitement of danger while posing no actual threat. It could also be that dinosaurs, from a child's point of view, seem like grown-ups, since they are both very old and very big.

By inspiring fantasy, dinosaurs alleviate a child's feelings of help-lessness. Gail Melson has described this vividly:

> A slight, shy, eight-year-old boy I know hurries home after school each day to go back to the age when dinosaurs roamed the Earth. A walking encyclopedia of dinosaur lore, he never tires of playing out battles between brontosaurus and tyran-nosaurus, using his six-inch high replicas. Unlike the power of adults or bigger, more assertive peers, dinosaur power is, literally, under his thumb.[1]

And why do most children leave that fascination behind well before reaching adulthood?

Adults often feel almost as powerless as children. They find relief in such activities as blasting aliens in video games, as well as other pastimes that are far less innocuous, but seldom in playing with dinosaurs. But maybe grown-ups don't really get over the dinosaur phase? It could be that they simply relive it vicariously through chil-dren. We have traditionally thought of dinosaurs as tragic, since (with the exception, we now know, of avians) they became extinct, yet were once enormously large and powerful. This corresponds to the

Carvings from Ta Prohm temple in Cambodia, built in 1186. The figure
looks uncannily like a stegosaurus. This might be due in part to a
discovery of dinosaur bones, but it is probably simply a coincidence.

combination of ability to dominate and extreme vulnerability, which
are both essential aspects of the way we think of humankind.

At any rate, that little boy is very far from being alone. At the
American Museum of Natural History in New York, which I visit
regularly, there is a shop in which almost an entire floor, one-third
of the space, is devoted to dinosaur paraphernalia, and most of the
items there have no more than a very oblique connection with science.
There are shelves upon shelves of plush dinosaur toys, many of which
are enormous. There are many picture books about dinosaurs, for
children that are just learning to read, mechanical dinosaurs and
countless accessories sporting pictures of dinosaurs.

That eight-year-old described by Melson could, in many ways, have been me, though palaeontology was not nearly so heavily commercialized in my childhood as it is today. Dinosaurs were, like presidents and teachers, accorded a lot of dignity. But in Chicago's Field Museum the reconstructed skeleton of an apatosaurus stood beneath the dome of a great hall. A huge bone was placed on a small pedestal in front of the skeleton, which people were invited to touch. When I did so, the bone seemed very hard and cold, almost metallic, but that only accented the metabolic warmth of the creature it had once helped to support. I was always a bit of a loner, as well as a romantic. Looking back, I suppose the world of dinosaurs was a sort of refuge for me, mostly from adults who thought they understood me yet never could.

There is something comforting for people of all ages about the way at least some kids in every generation go through a 'dinosaur phase',

Neolithic petroglyph in granite, dating from about 5,000–6,000 BCE, showing a creature that has an uncanny resemblance to a sauropod dinosaur. Lake Onega, Republic of Karelia.

A few of the dinosaur toys sold at the American Museum
of Natural History in New York.

despite all the changes that society has experienced in the last century
and a half. Dinosaurs appeal to a Victorian sort of 'childhood wonder',
as well as reassuring us that our childhood experiences are part of an
eternal condition. The phenomenon is especially remarkable because
it so often seems to first emerge spontaneously in children, with very
little adult encouragement. Yet perhaps dinosaurs, after all, are no
more immortal than human beings. The ways we imagine them, at
least, have been subject to constant change since their initial discovery
in the early nineteenth century.

Maybe, after my childhood encounter with dinosaur bones, every
subsequent experience of them could not be without a trace of disap-
pointment. For me, as a child, it was the gateway to a world that would
be without social pressures and demands. 'To be a dinosaur', a phrase
that I used in a late adolescent poem, meant simply to be myself. It
turns out, as this book will show, that dinosaurs, or at least their bones,
have been, since their discovery, deeply implicated in the worlds of
commerce and power politics. But my childhood experiences suggest
to me that, if all the hype could be finally stripped away, something
wonderful might remain.

The House on 79th Street...
where you can touch a dinosaur

Outside, it's just a big building on New York's West 79th Street. But step inside the American Museum of Natural History and the whole world is within walking distance. Here is the blazing sunlight of Africa with massive gorillas, lions, antelopes and eight magnificent elephants. In the Hall of North American Mammals, you can tour the National Parks and see among others, the mountain lion at Grand Canyon, the coyote at Yosemite and the grizzly at Yellowstone.

Here in a short afternoon, you can see how the American Indians used to live, you can study birdlife beneath brilliant Pacific skies, stroll along the ocean floor or visit the stars in the Hayden Planetarium. In Brontosaur Hall you look up at the 66-foot skeleton of the "Thunder Lizard" and look back over some 200,000,000 years.

You'll see actual dinosaur footprints found by a Sinclair-sponsored expedition, and run your fingers over a piece of fossilized bone, mounted on a pedestal for those who would like to touch a dinosaur.

America is a big land and rich in natural marvels. But for concentrated adventure and excitement, the building on 79th Street must be reckoned the most fascinating 23 acres in the world.

Free TOUR INFORMATION – If you would like to visit New York City or motor elsewhere in the U.S.A., the Sinclair Tour Service will help you plan your trip. Write: Tour Bureau, Sinclair Oil Corporation, 600 Fifth Avenue, New York 20, N. Y.

SINCLAIR Salutes the American Museum of Natural History

For adding to man's knowledge of the world he lives in, for making this knowledge a living and meaningful experience, and for demonstrating the importance of conservation of the natural wealth of our lands and wildlife.

SINCLAIR
A Great Name in Oil

An advertisement in *National Geographic Magazine* for Sinclair Oil and the American Museum of Natural History, 1956. Dinosaur bones displayed for people to touch were relatively common in museums until around the latter 1960s, when emphasis began to switch to audiovisual materials.

As Tom Rea has observed, since the early twentieth century people have thought of museums of natural history as 'temples to science, with the dinosaur exhibit as their central shrine'.[2] Museums, especially those of that era, were modelled on old temples or churches, with their high ceilings, domes and elaborate reliefs. They were, like churches, guardians of esoteric knowledge.

This resemblance of museums to cathedrals is not simply a matter of accidental associations. It reflects the ideas of natural theology, which was a driving force behind early science and, though challenged by evolutionary theory, remains very influential today. This holds that the order of the natural world is proof of a conscious plan and, thereby, the existence of God. To study this order is to reveal part of the divine plan, an activity that should inspire reverence and awe.

Religion linked the scientific communities with a larger public. In the words of Martin Rudwick,

> The popularization of science was formerly treated as a wholly one-way process . . . by which scientific pundits translated . . . their esoteric findings into more accessible language, with inevitable loss or distortion of content on the way. More recently, however, the process has come to be seen as being initiated as much from the 'popular' end as from the scientific.[3]

For one thing, science is dependent on sources of funding, which are heavily influenced by public perception. This, in turn, does much to determine the direction of research. Popularizations are also instrumental in recruiting young people to scientific vocations. In addition, scientists, whether they are conscious of it or not, cannot help but be influenced by the constant proliferation of images relating to their field in the popular media. In their capacities as employees of museums, companies and even universities, many scientists must constantly engage with the public, as representatives of their profession.

Furthermore, the way that scientists communicate with one another is now, inevitably, in large part through the popular media. Though professional journals continue to be important, they have always been slow and cumbersome. New discoveries are likely to be reported substantially before they can be written up in a formal way and subjected to peer review. The knowledge of a layperson may not compare in depth with that of a professional palaeontologist, but it can be almost as up to date. Accordingly, we will be better able to understand the significance of dinosaurs to the contemporary world if we do not think of science as monolithic, much less as a 'realm apart'. It would be more accurate to regard 'science' as a vast area of human endeavour, requiring not only researchers but philosophers, web designers, artists, teachers, journalists, museum professionals and so on. This contradicts the romantic image of the lone researcher engaged in a personal struggle for the truth, which will ultimately triumph over ignorance and superstition; an impression that is anachronistic at best. Today, most scientific papers have at least three authors, often many more. The connection to popular culture also limits the claim of science to objective truth, since it is intimately dependent on so many intangible, subjective, psychological and otherwise contingent factors.

Discoveries in physics are now almost impossible to visualize, even for researchers, but those in palaeontology are easily translated, with just a little imagination, into very colourful images. Within a very short time of their discovery in the late eighteenth and early nineteenth centuries, people had an emotional relationship with dinosaurs that was as complex, ambivalent, multifaceted and in some ways intimate as our bond with just about any living animal, including the dog and the cat. It was a relationship largely mediated by fantasy, like the relationship of the public to celebrities, yet no less authentic on that account. Dinosaurs have been featured in exhibitions, theme parks, novels, toys, movies, comics, logos and all the other paraphernalia of popular culture.

PLATE 8.

THE FOSSIL ELK
Edin.ʳ Roy: U. Museum.
Lizars sc.

Illustration from William Jardine, *The Naturalist's Library* (1840), showing the bones of an Irish elk. While the bones of dinosaurs and great mammals are indeed huge, researchers still regularly exaggerated their size. Perhaps some bones of dinosaurs were mixed with those of an elk in the model for this picture? It is more likely that the inflated size simply reflects the awe these animals evoked.

More overtly scientific activities are also pervaded by show-manship, though here it takes subtler forms. As will be explained in more detail later in this book, early discoverers of dinosaurs such as Gideon Mantell greatly exaggerated their size, appealing to the public's taste for both grandeur and novelty. In the late nineteenth and early twentieth centuries the search for huge bones became an arena of competition, for not only explorers but the industrialists and governments that backed them, and was, essentially, a form of trophy hunting.

Since, even with highly sophisticated tools, it is possible to infer only so much information from bones and related objects, those who wish to reconstruct the appearance and habits of dinosaurs have plenty of scope for imagination. Most popular representations of dinosaurs ignore even the limits imposed by palaeontology, while often incorporating a few recent discoveries in order to appear up to date. Our images of dinosaurs owe at least as much to the dragons and demons of medieval art – which, in turn, go back to archaic deities – as they do to fossils. These serpents were often associated with anachronistic beliefs or remote times, so dragon slayers such as St George or Beowulf, like palaeontologists of today, came across as promoters of modernity.

When were dinosaurs 'discovered'? Most scholars would say in the early nineteenth century. If one had to give a specific year, it might be 1824, when William Buckland named the megalosaurus. It might be 1842, when Richard Owen first coined the term 'dinosaur'. But most of the information that contributed to the idea of a 'dinosaur' had already been known for a very long time. As long as there have been human beings, they have, from time to time, come across dinosaur bones. They also have imagined huge reptilian creatures, somewhat analogous to those we call 'dinosaurs' today. But people had no analytic framework for describing dinosaurs, nor a cosmology in which to place them.

Bones

It now seems almost amazing that nobody, as far as we know, had even begun to study fossils as records of extinct animals until about the late eighteenth century, but the sort of reasoning that led to their identification was a good deal more complex than most people realize. We are now accustomed to thinking of them as imprints, usually incomplete and distorted, of living things, but, for those who lived a few hundred years ago, the remains of prehistoric creatures usually seemed to be just abstract patterns. What added a lot of confusion was the way the elements so often seem to mimic organic forms. Think of the faces, animals and palaces that people sometimes see in clouds or cracks in a plaster wall. Then there are dendrites, crystalline formations in rocks, which are often mistaken for fossil plants even today. Patterns in agate and other stones often appear uncannily like land- or seascapes.

A few bones, however, seemed so undisputably organic that they could not easily be attributed to the play of the elements. The basic form of bones has changed amazingly little from the age of dinosaurs or earlier until today. The sight of bones picked clean by predators was an everyday experience for human beings in the ancient world, but a few must have stood out dramatically by their size and weight. Dinosaur bones, especially, are often huge, often much larger than those of even the great mammals. Such bones, in much of the world at least, were probably once far more common and easily visible than they are today, just as they were in the western United States before settlement by Europeans. Many bones of dinosaurs and prehistoric mammals were doubtless destroyed by human settlements, exposed to and then worn down by weather, and ground up by practitioners of folk medicine. Then, in modern times, they were collected by palaeontologists and mostly put away in the basements of museums.

So why are there not far more references to such bones in the ancient world? It might be because they did not necessarily impress people as especially important. People did not make the modern distinction between the natural and supernatural worlds, and the existence of dragons and giants was usually taken for granted. The creatures that left those bones were long dead, so they posed no immediate threat, and there did not seem to be any great need to remark on them. But even without being explicitly mentioned, the enormous bones could have contributed to myths and legends.

Unidentified bones certainly had the power to inspire speculative, and often supernatural, ideas. At least since the Renaissance, narwhal horns were, throughout Europe, said to have belonged to unicorns, and could fetch enormous prices. Ostrich eggs were widely held to be those of griffins. But both of those were more common, in far better condition and much more easily recognizable than dinosaur bones. Large bones were generally said to be those of giants, which were the only creatures consistently credited with the vast scale of larger dinosaurs. Dragons, by contrast, particularly in the art of medieval and Renaissance Europe, may have had many features of dinosaurs, but they were rarely depicted as being larger than a crocodile or a lion. The Midgard Serpent of Norse mythology, the Chinese dragon and the dragon of the biblical Apocalypse are among the rare exceptions. It is only our knowledge of dinosaurs that, in the modern period, has moved us to think of dragons as enormous.

For about a century starting around 1200 BCE, nearly 3 tons of large bones collected from a river bed were venerated in an Egyptian temple as remains of the crocodile god Set.[4] In China, fossils that emerged in the Gobi Desert were known as 'dragon bones', and were ground up to provide an important ingredient in traditional medicine. They are mentioned in manuscripts dating from the third century CE, and there are also Chinese references to 'dragon teeth' by the sixteenth century. They were probably reasonably common, since elaborate procedures were laid out for their retrieval and preparation.[5] According to one theory, the griffin, which was often depicted by the ancient Greeks but has almost no role in their mythology, was originally a construction based on bones from Central Asia.[6]

In the early fifth century BCE, the Athenians built a shrine to Theseus, where enormous bones were venerated as his remains.[7] Giant bones in South Dakota that were exposed by storms were identified as either thunderbirds or their victims by Native Americans. Long before the arrival of Europeans, the Blackfoot people of what are now the Canadian provinces of Alberta and Saskatchewan believed that huge fossils were the ancestors of the buffalo. The Roman emperor Augustus placed a collection of enormous bones on public display, in what was perhaps one of the earliest museums.

In ancient Greece, huge bones were often held to be remains of titans or giants that had been vanquished by the gods. In the

American Northwest, the Sioux and other tribes had a very similar explanation for them. The giant bones were those of the Unktehi, monstrous reptilian creatures that had lived underground and been vanquished by the deities. Edward Cope and Charles Marsh, the pre-eminent fossil hunters of America in the late nineteenth century, both consulted with local tribes to learn where dinosaur bones might be found.

Many Asian monasteries have kept what are traditionally understood as dragon eggs, but which may, in some cases at least, come from dinosaurs.[8] In the Hindu temple complex of Pat Baba Mandir in west-central India, which is dedicated to the monkey god Hanuman, priests have kept bones and eggs of titanosaurs and other dinosaurs for many generations. The bones were believed to be those of demons that had been slain by the god Siva, and the spherical eggs were tokens of his presence.[9] The hosts of Ahriman in Zoroastrianism, the creations of Tiamat in Mesopotamian myth and even the evil armies in the biblical apocalypse also have many features of enormous serpents. The dragons killed by countless heroes from Perseus to St Margaret and St George are isolated creatures, which seemed to be remnants of a proverbial Age of Reptiles.

Possibly the first unequivocal reference to prehistoric bones appears in the *History* of Herodotus. In around 560 BCE the Spartans were engaged in a war with the Tegeans, and had been defeated several times. They sent a messenger to the oracle at Delphi, asking what they must do to prevail. The soothsayer told them that they must bring to Sparta the bones of the hero Orestes. A blacksmith in Tegea had once reported to a visiting Spartan that, while digging a well, he had found the bones of a giant about 7 cubits (approx. 6 m or 20 ft) in height. The Spartans decided that the giant was Orestes, and a team of them secretly entered Tegea, dug the bones up and brought them home.[10] Even these relics did not enable the Spartans to win a decisive victory, but they gained the initiative over the Tegeans, and the two city states finally became allies.

In the Middle Ages, bones were most often attributed to figures from pagan myths that had been absorbed into Christianity. Huge bones found in riverbeds were often ascribed to St Christopher, who was so mighty that, according to legend, he once carried the Christ Child, and thereby the weight of the world, across a stream during a tempest.[11] The saint was often depicted as a giant with the head of a dog, since he had been conflated with the Graeco-Egyptian deity Hermanubis, a Hellenized version of the canid-headed Egyptian guide to the dead. But the half-bestial identity might also have been suggested by bones of prehistoric creatures.

In *Genealogia deorum gentilium* (On the Genealogy of the Gods), first published in about 1374, Giovanni Boccaccio reports that three workers in Trapani, Sicily, who were digging the foundation of a house, discovered the entrance to an enormous cave, in which they saw a giant of about 60 metres (200 ft). They ran away, but returned with about three hundred villagers, who cautiously approached the titan. On being touched, the giant immediately disintegrated into dust, except for three huge teeth, part of a skull and a leg bone. The remains were placed on display in a local church.[12]

In the mid-fifteenth century, workers digging the foundation for an extension of St Stephen's Cathedral in Vienna dug up some enormous bones. These were placed on the main entrance, which became known as the 'giant's door'. According to legend, they belonged to titans who had assisted with the building of the original church, and had later been baptized.[13] The city of Klagenfurt in Austria kept the skull of a woolly rhinoceros in its town hall, believing that it was from a dragon that had been slain when the city was founded. In 1582 a sculptor made a bronze fountain in the image of this dragon, and

Byzantine icon of St Christopher with the head of a canid, painted in 17th-century Cappadocia and currently in the Byzantine and Christian Museum, Athens. St Christopher was regularly depicted as a giant and at times with a canine head. According to legend, he carried the Christ Child across a river during a raging storm. Both his enormous size and his visage may reflect the influence of prehistoric bones, perhaps even those of dinosaurs, revealed by violent weather.

Dragon Fountain in Klagenfurt, Austria, created in 1582 on the basis of an enormous skull that has since been identified as that of a woolly rhinoceros.

used the skull to model the creature's head.[14] In the sixteenth century, many enormous bones were found in the city of Worms, the legendary capital of Burgundy, where the hero Siegfried had been murdered. The bones were displayed in the marketplace as the remains of dragons and giants that the local champion had vanquished.[15]

There are many giant bones in the paintings of Hieronymus Bosch, which might be simply products of his inventive imagination but could also have been at least in part inspired by those of prehistoric creatures. One of the most puzzling instances is in the picture of Hell from the triptych *The Garden of Earthly Delights* (c. 1503–4). In the centre-left of the painting is a giant skull, which resembles that of a cow. To the right in the very centre of the painting is a demon-skeleton whose face looks directly out at the viewer. The legs of the monster resemble tree trunks, except for being completely white and having a large bend between the calf and the thigh. The torso is an enormous eggshell, with a large opening through which we see people seated as though in a tavern. On the head, a wide brim, on which demons march sinners about, is crowned with massive bagpipes.[16] It is possible that this figure could be an imaginative reconstruction of a prehistoric skeleton. The eggshell body, particularly, could have been suggested by innumerable skeletal fragments.

An engraving attributed to Bosch's younger Venetian contemporaries Marcantonio Raimondi and/or his student Agostino Veneziano entitled *The Witches' Procession* (c. 1520) shows a more plausible reconstruction of a dinosaur. The scene is a witches' sabbath, in which two figures are pulling along a complete skeleton of a monster, ridden by a witch. At first glance, we could even take the bones for those of a sauropod dinosaur, but the details are fanciful. Beside the giant frame is a smaller skeleton of a sort of infernal unicorn, ridden by another witch.[17] The picture might be a fantasy, but one detail, especially, suggests a scientific aspiration behind it. In the far right, a man is trying to figure out how two huge bones fit together, much as a palaeontologist might do.

In 1613, construction workers in Dauphiné, a province in southeastern France, reportedly came upon some enormous bones in a tomb inscribed with the name 'Teutobochus'. Teutobochus was a huge German chieftain who, according to Roman historians, had been captured by the armies of the Roman general Marius. Then, in 1618, Jean Riolan, a physician, published an essay entitled 'Geantologie' (Giantology), in which he claimed that no human beings so large had ever existed, and the bones must be those of another creature. That same year, the distinguished surgeon Nicholas Habicot replied that such humans did indeed exist, as attested since ancient times by many writers, and that, furthermore, the bones did not resemble those of any known animal. Several other distinguished anatomists and historians joined in the debate, which continued for a couple

Hieronymus Bosch, detail showing a giant jawbone in Hell in *The Garden of Earthly Delights*, *c.* 1503–4, oil on oak panel. This could be a cow's jaw, except for the enormous scale. But what might such a 'cow' have looked like when alive?

Hieronymus Bosch, detail showing the 'tree man' in Hell, from *The Garden of Earthly Delights*, c. 1503–4, oil on oak panel. The scene takes place deep underground, and the huge figure in the centre may be a very early attempt to reconstruct a prehistoric creature on the basis of bones.

of centuries,[18] before a consensus was reached that the animal had been a prehistoric creature, probably a giant sloth. We could today, of course, determine this with near certainty, but the bones have been lost.

Through most of the early modern period, enormous bones continued to be usually, though not invariably, attributed to giants. One other possibility often mentioned by early scientists in Europe is that they might be bones of elephants brought over by Hannibal or even the Romans. The earliest discovered bone that may, with any confidence, be attributed to a dinosaur was discussed by Robert Plot in his *Natural History of Oxfordshire*, first published in 1677. He tells of having dug up a fragment, weighing about 8 kilograms (20 lb), of an enormous thigh bone in the Parish of Cornwell. He considered that it might have been that of an elephant, but added that a proportionally even larger bone had been found in the ruins of St Mary Woolchurch after the Great Fire of London in 1666 and was later placed on display at a tavern in Kent. He considered it highly unlikely that an elephant would have been buried in a church, though it was possible that the church might have been erected on the ruins of a pagan temple. He went on to argue, using examples from biblical times to his own era, that people could obtain enormous stature. After a detailed discussion, he concluded that it was the bone of a man or woman. The bone has not survived, but a meticulously drawn illustration in his book indicated to later palaeontologists that the creature was a megalosaurus. Plot mentions several similar bones, dug up by others, which he had seen, so perhaps coming across the bones of dinosaurs was not uncommon at the time.

The Swiss scientist Johann Jakob Scheuchzer claimed in 1726 to have found, at Oningen near Baden in Switzerland, a relatively complete fossil skeleton of a person who had lived before the great Flood – when Noah saved the animals in his ark – whose fate he held up as a warning for his contemporaries. He called it *Homo diluvii testis* or 'Man Who Was Witness to the Flood'.[19] An inveterate moralist,

Agostino Veneziano and/or Marcantonio Raimondi, *The Witches' Procession*, or
The Carcass, c. 1520, engraving. Even if the skeletons here may be fanciful, the picture
suggests that scientists were at least starting to conceive the project of reconstructing
prehistoric creatures from their bones. The man on the right is trying
to fit two bones together.

he described it as 'A most rare memorial of that accursed generation
of men of the first world, the skeleton of a Man Drowned in the
Flood'.[20] In the German edition of his later work *Physica sacra* (Sacred
Physics, published 1731), also called the *Kupfer-Bibel* (Copper Bible),
he included a couplet about the fossil by Pastor Johann Martin Miller,
which was translated into English by Herbert Wendt as:

> Afflicted skeleton of old, doomed to damnation,
> Soften, thou stone, the hearts of this wicked generation.[21]

The skeleton was only slightly over 90 centimetres (3 ft) long
and had no obvious resemblance to a human being. Scheuchzer
was, among other things, a doctor who had lectured on anatomy,
but the head had little similarity to a human one, and it was much
too large in proportion to the body. In the early nineteenth century,
Georges Cuvier identified the fossil as being that of a giant prehistoric

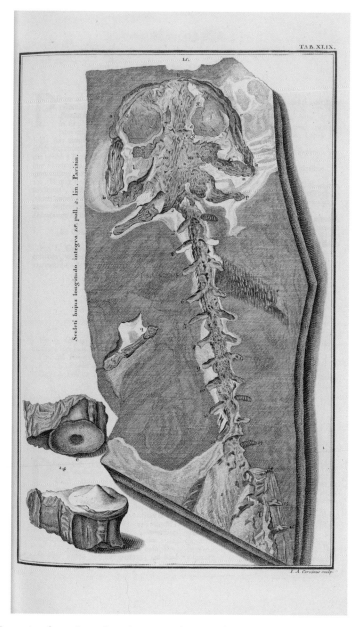

Illustration from the early 18th century showing what Johann Scheuchzer thought were the bones of *Homo diluvii testis*, a sinner who perished in the great Flood; they were later identified as those of a giant salamander.

Illustration to Johann Scheuchzer, *Physica sacra* (1731). This illustration, showing the creation of Adam, shows how Scheuchzer and others blended biblical lore with natural history. The first man is mystically formed out of light, but the landscape in the background is shown in a very naturalistic style. The embryos in the foreground represent generations to come, and they are weeping at the fate that awaits them.

salamander, and people have laughed at Scheuchzer for his mistake ever since.

Fossilized bones had previously often been attributed to giants, but Scheuchzer's find, if it had indeed been human, would have to have either been of a child, an idea that Scheuchzer repeatedly rejected, or else a dwarf. Scheuchzer could not have identified the bones as those of a 'dinosaur' or any other sort of prehistoric animal, since the necessary concepts were not available. Furthermore, he believed that all fossils had been created during Noah's Flood, neither before nor afterwards. He may have thought that the figure had, through depravity, degenerated from the human form, in much the way that, according to tradition, the fallen angels had become bestial. In that event, it was a warning that human status should not be taken for granted, but might be lost through wickedness.

Scheuchzer was enormously learned, insatiably curious and very imaginative, yet unscientific in his methods and careless about details. In a plate from *Physica sacra* showing two primates and a peacock imported from exotic lands by King Solomon, he presented a skeleton in a way that was even more speculative, yet oddly prophetic of dinosaurs. Scheuchzer delighted in complex allegories, involving both scientific observation and biblical texts, and this one is particularly difficult to interpret. The simians are exchanging intense gazes underneath a date tree, in a way suggestive of Adam and Eve in the Garden of Eden. One is clearly a chimpanzee; the other looks unmistakably like a baboon, yet is identified a bit equivocally in the text as a 'meerkatze'. That term now refers to prairie dogs, but at that time usually designated any primate or analogous animal transported on a ship.

Above the primates is a large insert showing a skeleton. According to the text, it is that of a 'meerkatze', but it actually looks nothing like that of a baboon or any other primate. The skeleton is standing completely, and even ecstatically, erect, looking up at the sky. Its backbone, however, extends into a long tail, like that of a lizard but completely unlike that of any primate, which gives it the support necessary to stay upright. The hind legs, despite the erect posture, look as if they normally projected perpendicularly from the spine. The forelimbs are stretched out and pointed downwards, suggesting that they do not have the flexibility of arms. The entire figure seems awkward yet oddly triumphant.

The front of the skull is almost completely flat, with no trace of a snout, and is reminiscent of *Homo diluvii testis*. Just possibly, this might be an attempted reconstruction of the old sinner, incorporating fossilized bones that Scheuchzer had found elsewhere – he was the proud owner of one of the largest fossil collections in the world. The illustration shows a biblical scene that is placed chronologically after the Flood, but it may be that Scheuchzer, like many people in premodern times, regarded apes as degenerate human beings, rather like *Homo diluvii testis*. Scheuchzer was an eccentric, but also a visionary. Except perhaps for the skull, the skeleton prefigures nineteenth-century reconstructions of dinosaurs such as the iguanodon.

Scheuchzer's depiction could be dismissed as something like science fiction, but the same thing could be said of just about all writing about dinosaurs up through the present. People seem impelled to construct relatively complete images of them, but they must do so on the basis of evidence that, however sophisticated, is extremely fragmentary and incomplete. They can only attempt the task through the relatively uninhibited use of fantasy and intuition.

The idea of a distinct world of children is primarily a Victorian creation, dating to approximately the same time as the discovery of dinosaurs. Abetted by the rise of capitalism, which impelled companies to seek new markets, children were given their own rooms, styles, legends, customs and, perhaps most importantly, books. The general rule was that realism was for adults, while fantasy was for kids. Dinosaurs bridged that gap, since images of them incorporated a great deal of both.

As I will endeavour to show in this book, Scheuchzer's error inaugurates an archetypal pattern that runs through the study of

TAB. CCCCLXII.

I. REG. Cap. X. v. 11. 12. 22.   I. Buch der Kön. Cap. X. v. 11. 12. 22.
Simia, Cercopithecus, Pavo.   Affen, Meerkatzen und Pfauen.

I. A. Fridrich sculps.

dinosaurs up to the present. We still regard them in a sense as almost human, as 'old sinners that lived before the Flood'. To put it another way, dinosaurs provide the foremost template in the natural world for thinking about human destiny. We are not descended from dinosaurs, and our ancestors did not interact with them, outside of comic books and B-movies. But, precisely for those reasons, it is easier to consider their world as a mirror of the human condition.

The fact that dinosaurs became extinct has made their story resonate with the apocalyptic traditions of the Zoroastrian, Judaic, Christian and Islamic religions. Their size and power suggest empires and battles on an epic scale, perhaps even a sort of Armageddon. Even the current view that some dinosaurs survived to become birds suggests a sort of angelic elect that will be saved. But our apocalyptic fears have been secularized, and the meaning of dinosaurs has changed with them. In the late nineteenth and early twentieth centuries, dinosaurs were often used to represent big business, though their eventual demise could seem like a proletarian revolution. Later, their apocalyptic associations might be used to express terror of a nuclear holocaust or of ecological collapse. In addition to the elemental appeal of great size and antiquity, the reason for the popularity of dinosaurs is that their symbolism is flexible enough to accommodate a vast range of meanings. They have been used to comment on human violence, innocence, wealth, industrialization, failure, modernity, tragedy, extinction and far more.

But none of these things really has much to do with dinosaurs in the end. We are simply imposing our own meanings on their endlessly mysterious lives. I will not preach against this, for exploiting other

Illustration to Johann Scheuchzer, *Physica sacra* (1731). The picture may contain an allegorical meaning which has since become obscure. The skeleton above may be a reconstruction of what Scheuchzer took for an old sinner who had perished in the Flood, and it combines human and simian features with an extended tail. The figure in the foreground on the left appears to be a baboon, while the one on the right is a chimpanzee, except for its tail. Sitting beneath a tree and gazing into each other's eyes, they suggest Adam and Eve.

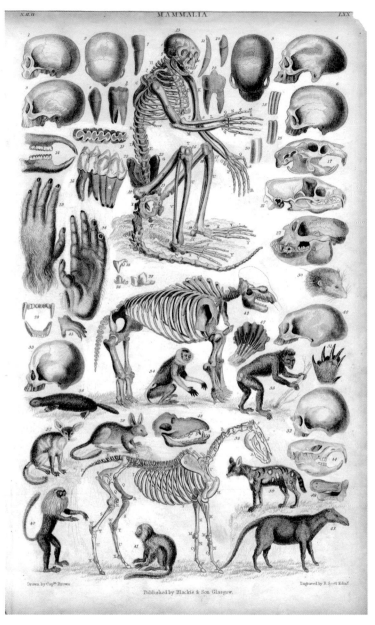

Bones of prehistoric creatures including a hominid, from a British book of natural history published in the mid-19th century. At the time this graphic was produced, fragmentary bones of the Neanderthal man had been found, but the figure had not been thoroughly described or identified. The picture gives him a tail, similar to that of Scheuchzer's 'old sinner', perhaps simply because a tail was associated with 'savagery'.

creatures as symbols is simply what human beings do, and I am no more exempt than anyone else. But, when we speak of dinosaurs essentially as cultural artefacts, we should remember, from time to time, that they were once, and still are, vastly more.

The house of bones

The entire range of modern responses to dinosaurs is depicted in Tony Sarg's lithograph of the American Museum of Natural History (AMNH) in 1927. The artist was a German-American puppeteer and illustrator in the early twentieth century who is best known for designing the first helium balloons for Macy's Thanksgiving Day Parade, such as Felix the Cat and Toy Soldier, in 1927. His picture of the AMNH is one of a series of lithographs that he produced in the 1920s showing various iconic places in New York City. This was the decade known as the Roaring Twenties, when New York was often celebrated, and sometimes reviled, as the epitome of modernity, with big business, big buildings and even big dinosaurs. Sarg's lithographs show none of our rather stereotyped ideas of the era such as flappers or bootleggers. Instead, they depict everyday people who, often oblivious to such iconic locations as the Empire State Building or the Chrysler Building, follow their own quirky agendas.

The picture shows the hall where skeletons of dinosaurs and other prehistoric creatures are displayed, most prominently an apatosaurus and a tyrannosaurus, illustrating the combination of awe, perplexity and curiosity with which the bones of these creatures were regarded. It also records how even these feelings could not hold people's attention for very long. Near the centre of the picture is a uniformed guide who is lecturing and, a little pretentiously, pointing to a case with three tyrannosaurus skulls. He has an attentive, if rather small, audience: a little girl with her doll who looks up at him, ignoring the dinosaurs. A short distance away, one well-dressed gentleman, with his hat on the ground, may be acting out the behaviour of a dinosaur, while his companion looks on critically. To their left, a mischievous little boy has got an older girl to chase him by snatching her hat. Two men in military uniform are practising their drills. On a bench in the background, two other men, possibly vagrants, are drowsing. As in all of Sarg's lithographs, it is our constant proneness to distraction, even in the presence of the most august monuments like dinosaur skeletons, that makes us 'human'.

The apatosaurus, the largest dinosaur known at the time, in the left-centre of the page seems wiser than the men and women. Dinosaurs had two openings in their skulls known as the antorbital fenestrae, between the nostrils and the eyes. In this case, each has a point at the bottom, where light and shadow pass through the skull, forming a white spot that resembles the pupil of an eye, through which the dinosaur surveys the scene. Just below, a man bends over reading a sign that tells about the dinosaur bones, while the apatosaurus seems to gaze down at him. Here, the human beings come across as something of a mysterious natural phenomenon, while the dinosaurs, especially the apatosaurus, have the dignity of monumental statues. One has the impression that the apatosaurus, and perhaps other dinosaurs as well, may be quietly laughing at us.

People in the modern era have continually been haunted by a feeling that their lives are petty and trivial, consumed by things like small talk and bureaucratic details. They are bourgeois, boring, unheroic and unadventurous. We constantly long for great passion, devotion, conflict, piety, wickedness and danger. We are nostalgic less for periods of peace and prosperity than for eras of high drama, from the Jerusalem of Solomon to the empire of Alexander. Part of the reason we are drawn so to wild animals is that their lives, in which the prospect of death is never far away, seem to have a drama and an immediacy that is lacking in our own. As Helen Macdonald

Tony Sarg, lithograph showing the dinosaurs at the American Museum of Natural History, 1927. The dinosaurs here seem to evoke a momentary awe in some visitors, but most people are very easily distracted by other concerns.

LA GIRAFFE.

Illustration showing a giraffe from the Comte de Buffon's *Histoire naturelle* (1786). When this picture was made, giraffes had been viewable in Paris zoos for about half a century. The exaggerated size and heft of this one may reflect the discovery of dinosaur bones.

has put it, 'We use animals as ideas to amplify and enlarge aspects of ourselves, turning them into simple, safe harbors for things we feel and often cannot express.'[22] Dinosaurs, especially, seem to have lived, in so many senses, on an enormous scale, and we seem to partake of that splendour through association with them.

John Margolies, Rebel Yell Raceway dinosaur statue, Route 441, Pigeon Forge, Tennessee. The 'rebel yell' was a shout used by Confederate soldiers in the American Civil War as they charged into battle, which some scholars have speculated may go back to a Celtic battle cry. Here it is identified with the putative roar of a *Tyrannosaurus rex*.

CHAPTER II

How Dragons Became Dinosaurs

> . . . And, when night
> Darkens the streets, then wander forth the sons
> Of Belial, flown with insolence and wine.
>
> JOHN MILTON, *Paradise Lost*

'If a tree falls in a forest and no one is around to hear it, does it make a sound?' This philosophical thought experiment has been discussed, with variations in wording, in college classes over the past couple of centuries. What if, instead of a tree falling in the forest, it is a tyrannosaurus that roars in a vanished world? If nobody is around to name it, is the creature really a tyrannosaurus? And is the sound really a roar? When we even describe such a creature, the existence of a hypothetical human observer is implied. We are making human measurements, appealing to human senses, using human categories and following human agendas. You might even say that the imaginary witness is a sort of colonist, preparing what Martin Rudwick has called 'deep time' – the aeons in which the human race did not yet exist – for civilization. Today, the study of events in deep time is routine, and we forget how difficult this was to comprehend at the start of the modern era. Whatever might happen before human creation was then conceived in a rather dreamlike way, as largely outside time.

Today, it is hard for us to appreciate just how strange the idea of enormous, prehistoric beasts appeared to educated Europeans around the start of the nineteenth century. These creatures would have been easier to comprehend for people of antiquity or the Middle Ages, who were accustomed to tales of the supernatural, and easier still for Asians, who traditionally thought in terms of vast expanses of time. They would not have seemed especially counter-intuitive to the early alchemists, for whom dragons symbolized the spiritualization of earthly substance. But the literal thinking implicit in both science and religious fundamentalism had, in many ways, structured the European imagination to a point where dinosaurs and other inhabitants of deep time had become very hard to envision.

Suppose that a contemporary person travelled back in time, carrying a picture of *Tyrannosaurus rex*, reconstructed according to the latest research, perhaps with brightly coloured feathers covering its body. She tries to explain the image to a highly educated clergyman of the seventeenth century. The host from another era would at first suppose that the creature depicted was either imaginary or else currently alive. If our contemporary told her host that the tyrannosaurus lived 65 million years ago but then disappeared, she would meet with perplexity. Chronological dating of events in deep time did not become possible until radiocarbon testing was discovered in the early twentieth century. It is highly unlikely that our time traveller could explain our contemporary ideas of time, since they are so closely tied to concepts of physics that, even today, remain hard for most people to understand. What would come across is that the dinosaurs lived long, long ago in something like the realm of fairy tales.

Dinosaurs – in the sense of giant, primeval, lizard-like creatures, with features of many birds and mammals – have haunted the human imagination from time immemorial. The study of dinosaurs channelled the ancient tradition of composite monsters, which goes back at least to the beginning of what we call 'civilization'. It drew heavily on the iconography of demons, grotesques, demigods and creatures reported by explorers in (for Europeans) exotic lands. The emerging field of palaeontology gave the composite creatures a new name and placed them in a remote period of time, but it left them in some ways not greatly changed.

Dinosaurs are, and have always been, essentially dragons, and these have by no means always appeared negative. The Asian dragon is a bringer of rain and a symbol of primordial energy. The alchemical dragon represented transformative power. A dragon is the symbol of Wales, and many noble houses have included dragons on their coats of arms. Images of dinosaurs also owed much to travellers' tales of enormous snakes and other fantastic creatures in remote parts of the world, which were already fairly common in the Middle Ages and Renaissance and continued unabated as the British Empire expanded.

Dragons, particularly Western ones, are constantly associated with elemental powers that ruled in a primordial era: for early Mesopotamians, children of the goddess-demon Tiamat; for the Greeks, the titans; for the Norse, the frost giants; for Christians, pagan divinities. As David Gilmore has put this,

> monsters have always carried with them the whiff of a remote and distant past, either morphologically in an atavistic appearance, or metaphorically through some chronological inversion (e.g., T. rex). So, in the same enigmatic way as in ancient Egypt and Greece, monsters are still symbolically ancestral to humanity, dredging into consciousness some deep-seated hint of superseded, archaic times.[1]

When a hero such as Cadmus or St George killed a dragon, the deed marked the end of an old era and the beginning of a new one.

In many respects, dinosaurs became cultural successors to the dragons of legend, but the modern idea of a 'dinosaur' could not even be articulated until the nineteenth century. It required a very

Hieronymus Bosch, detail of *The Garden of Eden*, from the triptych *The Garden of Earthly Delights*, *c.* 1503–4, oil on panel. Christian tradition had generally held that there had been no predation in Eden, but Bosch, despite being intensely religious, depicts animals there eating one another. Even more significantly, he shows a sort of evolution: the animals begin in water and then emerge gradually, taking on forms closer to those that are familiar to us today.

Ouroboros, from Abraham Eleazar, *Uraltes Chymisches Werk* (Leipzig, 1760). The serpent or dragon with its tail in its mouth is an ancient Egyptian motif and appears frequently in alchemical and esoteric literature as a symbol of eternity.

intricate organization of experience, particularly of time, in which dinosaurs could occupy a niche. First, time had to be conceived as more unequivocally linear. Next, it was necessary to divide time into distinct eras. This was done at first with historical time, and then, very gradually, with prehistory. The chronology of the world gradually widened and became more precise, until a segment could eventually be marked off as the 'Age of Dinosaurs'. Finally, it was necessary to recognize that dinosaurs had become extinct.

The Hindu deity Krishna dancing on the head of the serpent Kaliya,
early 20th-century illustration. One of the many images in which civilization
is represented by triumph over a reptilian adversary.

The discovery of deep time

There are many alternative ways to think about time. Asian religious traditions such as Hinduism and Buddhism view change as an illusion. Modern physics views time as a dimension analogous to space, an idea that has, through the influence of science fiction, largely been assimilated into popular culture. Superstring theory, which views the world as existing in not four but ten or more dimensions, opens at least theoretical possibilities of time travel through 'wormholes'. As The Doctor said in an episode of the science fiction show *Doctor Who* entitled 'Blink', we may think 'that time is a strict progression of cause to effect, but actually . . . it is more like a big ball of wibbly wobbly timey wimey . . . stuff'.

A view of time as linear is an inheritance of the great monotheistic religions: Zoroastrianism, Judaism, Christianity and Islam. In all of them, history leads up to an apocalyptic conflict of good and evil, which will end in a renewal of the earth and redemption for the just. Even in this tradition, however, there are cyclic elements. In the Bible, the old world is destroyed by a great flood, after which God announces to Noah a new covenant with humankind, effectively creating the world once again. The appearance of Christ, for his followers, marks yet another stage in the relations between man and God, and Jesus became known as 'the New Adam'.

The Western, linear conception of time is an exception among human cultures. The default perception of time, to which people have been perpetually reverting, is 'eternalism', the belief that the world is essentially what it has always been, while any change is superficial. This is suggested by the natural rhythms of the seasons, of day and night, and of birth and death. Some cultures do not have a creation myth, and those that do often place the beginning of the world outside of time. For indigenous Australians, it is the Dream Time, of which current reality is only a reiteration. Hinduism and related religions divide time into vast epochs, which may last for millions of years, but eternally recur. The creation myth of the Navajo people tells of four worlds prior to our own, inhabited by beings that were partly human yet resembled insects, swallows, grasshoppers and mirages, a bit like the stages into which palaeontologists divide the evolution of living things.[2]

Most of the narrative in the *Theogony* of the Greek poet Hesiod, writing in the eighth century BCE, takes place in deep time, before the appearance of humankind. In many ways, it seems remarkably modern. It is full of geological upheavals, fantastic creatures, cosmic wars, tempests and volcanoes. Geology and weather are anything but stable, and forms of life also undergo perpetual change.[3] What differentiates Hesiod's view from the modern one is, above all, his lack of chronology. The events in his narrative such as the war between gods and giants are never dated; in fact even the sequence of events is not very clear.

Even as people in the Western world began to construct linear histories, much of experience remained apart from them. Until the modern era, a history of the natural world would have seemed inconceivable. Even common people seemed to be largely outside of history. It was mostly an affair of kings, generals, battles and dominions. In medieval paintings of ancient events, people are shown wearing contemporary dress and using current weapons. Alexander the Great, for example, might be shown as a knight in armour with a jousting lance in hand. There was little sense of people in previous times belonging to a different era, with appropriate customs, clothes, technologies and so on.

The discovery of dinosaurs in the eighteenth and nineteenth centuries required a fundamental change in the Western perception of time, which became far more expansive. Archbishop Ussher of Armagh had calculated in the mid-seventeenth century on the basis of biblical accounts that the cosmos began in the year 4004 BCE. He also put together a detailed chronology of all events in the Bible. In many family Bibles printed over the next couple of centuries, these dates were placed in the margins. What was innovative here was not the specific chronology but the idea that such events might be dated at all. Previously, the predominant view of time had been far more sensuous, experiential and dependent on visual imagination. In the early modern period, ideas about time became increasingly abstract, and people thought of days and years as objective structures.

In the sixteenth century, Europeans still looked to the biblical Book of Genesis for their basic account of the world's origin, but probably proportionally fewer were fundamentalists than today. Literal accuracy was not yet very sharply distinguished from symbolic or philosophical truth. The Book of Genesis came to be considered a historical as well as a religious document, the only record of the events near the beginning of the world. Careful readers of the Bible realized that God did not create the sun and moon, separating day and night, until the fourth day of creation. They rightly inferred that the six days of creation were not necessarily of 24 hours each, but of indefinite duration. The 'days' were stages in the emergence of the cosmos, each of which might have lasted for an entire era.

Tradition, bolstered by a few biblical allusions to demons such as Azazel, made the major event before the creation of Adam the defeat of Satan and his minions. Pieter Brueghel the Elder's *The Fall of the Rebel Angels* (1562) shows a sort of evolution 'in reverse'.[4] The angels appear, except for their wings, as idealized human beings. As the rebel angels are expelled from Heaven and plummet towards Hell they become far more diverse, even fantastic, taking on features of reptiles, insects, molluscs, fish, amphibians and apes. The fall of the rebels from Heaven was an early version of evolution. The degenerated angels in Abrahamic tradition provided an initial template for the concept of dinosaurs. But this was evolution as deterioration, and the nineteenth century understood evolution as progress.

The most common image of such a transformation is the serpent of Eden, which in the Bible was cursed by God to glide on its belly in the dust. Such a punishment implied that the serpent had once

Pieter Breughel the Elder, *The Fall of the Rebel Angels*, 1562, oil on panel. As the minions
of Satan fall to earth, they lose their essentially human form and become more bestial
and fantastic. Most especially, they take on features of insects, reptiles, fish
and crustaceans.

walked upright. This is, at least considered as an image, in line with
evolutionary theory, which holds that snakes evolved from lizards that
had lost their legs. The upright serpent before the Fall was imagined
in many ways during the Middle Ages and early modern periods, and
in some it bore a remarkable resemblance to dinosaurs.

Especially in popular culture, Satan is the grandfather of *Tyrannosaurus rex*. The giant therapod allegedly rules the dinosaurs, much
as the Devil governs the rebel angels. We can still see the paradigm
of Milton at work in the way *Tyrannosaurus rex* is thought of, and
named, as a 'tyrant king'. The early images of dinosaurs, with their

TAB XXIX.

GENESIS Cap. III. v. 7.
Ficus Folium Nuditatis Tegmen.

I. Buch Mosis Cap. III. v. 7.
Das Feigenblatt ein Decke vor die Blöße.

H. Sperling sculp.

Illustration to Johann Scheuchzer's *Physica sacra* (1731) showing Adam and Eve.
Alongside a literal rendering of the biblical story of Adam and Eve, the illustration
shows close scientific observation.

reptilian features, were, in part unconsciously, based on demons from Renaissance and early modern depictions, and this legacy is far from exhausted.

Transience

In Shakespeare's play *As You Like It*, one of the characters states that the world is almost 6,000 years old (IV.I), which was the predominant view in Elizabethan times. Shakespeare may well have shared it, though there are indications to the contrary in his work. I suspect that he, as well as some of his more sensitive contemporaries, had an intuition of geographic time, even though the concept had not yet been fully articulated, and that was part of the reason why they were so preoccupied with transience.

Shakespeare, writing around the end of the sixteenth century, made several references to the vast scale of geological time, particularly in his sonnets, for example number 64:

> When I have seen by Time's fell hand defaced
> The rich proud cost of outworn buried age;
> When sometime lofty towers I see down-razed,
> And brass eternal slave to mortal rage;
> When I have seen the hungry ocean gain
> Advantage on the kingdom of the shore,
> And the firm soil win of the wat'ry main,
> Increasing store with loss, and loss with store;
> When I have seen such interchange of state,
> Or state itself confounded to decay;
> Ruin hath taught me thus to ruminate, –
> That Time will come and take my love away.
> The thought is as a death, which cannot choose
> But weep to have that which it fears to lose.[5]

The first four lines are focused on historical time, specifically the rise and fall of mighty civilizations, but the next five expand the scope to include geographical time as well. In the last five, Shakespeare talks of his own life, which seems at once endlessly small and important.

Dinosaurs would not be studied for a few hundred years, but, just for fun, let us try interpreting the poem with reference to them. Let us say that the 'outworn buried age' is the Age of Dinosaurs. We can pretend the 'lofty towers' refers to their great size, and the 'brass' to their bones. Of course, that is not what the author intended, but the poem still makes good sense, and its basic meaning is not greatly changed. The dinosaurs were magnificent, and their demise reminds us that all things are transient, the great theme of lyric poetry.

The lost paradise

The work which, more than any other, opened deep time to human investigation is the poem *Paradise Lost* (1667–74) by John Milton, an epic telling of the fall of the rebel angels and the temptation in the Garden of Eden. It established the remote past as a place for intricate narratives, helped to prepare the public imaginatively for the discovery of dinosaurs and even articulated some of the paradigms by which we visualize dinosaurs to this day. Milton filled the time before Adam and Eve with vast numbers of both angels and devils. He at least partially 'humanized' both, giving them names and individual personalities. *Paradise Lost* is full of grandiose conflicts, theatrical gestures, awesome pageantry. In its emphasis on burning lakes, tempests and natural catastrophes, it anticipated the vision of later scientists, particularly the catastrophism of Cuvier.

In *Paradise Lost*, Satan, having just taken the form of a serpent to engineer the temptation of Eve and the subsequent expulsion of her and Adam from Paradise, returns to Pandemonium, the realm of devils. He announces his victory, expecting great applause, but is surprised to hear hissing instead. God has changed him and the other

Illustration to Johann Scheuchzer's *Physica sacra* (1731) showing the serpent of Eden, with modern snakes in the foreground. In the Bible the serpent is set apart from other animals by possessing the ability to speak. The one here could almost be a dinosaur.

Gustave Doré, illustration to Milton's *Paradise Lost*, 1866. The angelic host at war with rebels patrols a craggy, mountainous landscape before a distant horizon.

Gustave Doré, illustration to Milton's *Paradise Lost*, 1866. Satan has boasted
to his minions about taking the form of a snake to seduce Eve. He expected
applause but hears hissing instead, for God has changed him and the other
devils into serpents.

demons into serpents.[6] As the realm of deep time began to open up
in the early modern period, what initially filled it was not prehistoric
animals but demons and rebel angels. One could almost say that the
devils turned into dinosaurs. Since the adventure of humankind was
by then well under way in his poem, Milton no longer felt he had to
depict devils in such anthropomorphic terms, and to do so would

have detracted from human exceptionalism. Well into the nineteenth century, writers on prehistoric creatures would not infrequently mention Milton.

Thomas Hawkins, the owner of one of the best fossil collections in Britain and a respected member of the London Geological Society,

Gustave Doré, illustration to Milton's *Paradise Lost*, 1866. Satan clings to a rocky cliff, very likely of limestone, of the sort that would later inspire early geologists and palaeontologists. Note that his wings now resemble those of a bat rather than a bird.

shows the influence of Milton in *The Book of the Great Sea-dragons,
Ichthyosauri and Plesiosauri* (1840). At a time when palaeontology was
still a novelty, he cited *Paradise Lost* to show how divine beings
vanquished the rebel angels. He went on to say,

> and the bones of these great Sea-dragons, plesiosauri, are the
> remains of but one of the vile Colonies from Tophet (Moloch),
> which Jehovah visited with wrath, and swept out of the World
> in a whirlwind of fury and Indignation forever. Each and
> every one of the kingdoms accursed shall be destroyed in
> like manner, and the arch-ruler thereof driven at last to his

Illustration to *The Primitive World* (1857) by Adolphe François Pannemaker. Like many
illustrations from the early to mid-19th century, this one places bloody scenes of
predation against fiery skies of an apocalyptic landscape. The implication is that God
is punishing the primeval creatures for their savagery.

remaining Citadel in the human heart, be cast out even thence into perdition everlasting.[7]

For Hawkins, the primeval lizards were indeed remnants of an earlier period in earth's history, but they were not necessarily prehistoric or even fully extinct. His work may be the first articulation of the fantasy, which remains ubiquitous today, that giant saurians once lived alongside human beings.

But perhaps the greatest influence of Milton was on how people visualized events in deep time. At the time he composed *Paradise Lost*, Milton was blind, but the poem relies to an extraordinary extent on visual evocation. The rhythms of his blank verse are stately and majestic, yet without much variation. All characters including Satan, God the Father, Jesus Christ, Adam and Eve speak with the same cadences, syntax and vocabulary. But the poem's emotional power lies primarily in the way its story unfolds as a series of hallucinatory images. These are never the sort of pictures that rely on close observation, but, rather, those of a cosmic imagination, ranging freely across vast expanses of space and time.

The first illustrated edition of *Paradise Lost*, engraved by Michael Burgesse after, in some instances at least, designs by John Baptiste de Medina, already established the tradition of small figures in melo-dramatic poses framed by expansive landscapes, featuring darkened clouds, heavenly bodies, rocky outcrops and dense vegetation. None of these conventions was by itself unprecedented. For about two centuries, Flemish artists had depicted religious scenes against vast landscapes, showing the presence of God through the grandeur of his creation, for example the way light fell through the trees. The backgrounds were often painted with as much care, and seemed as full of divine significance, as the human figures. But the illustrations to *Paradise Lost* established conventions for thinking about stories that took place long before the appearance of mankind. The basic formula of Burgesse was followed by other illustrators of the epic, such as

John Baptiste de Medina, illustration to Milton's *Paradise Lost*, 1688.
The Angel Gabriel is showing Adam the future that will result from
his disobedience to God. Already, in the first illustrated edition of Milton's
poem, we see the harsh, expansive, rocky landscapes that will be used
by painters as backgrounds in scenes that are remote in time.

John Martin, William Blake and Gustave Doré, over the next two
centuries. Perhaps coincidentally, the drama of Adam's Fall was set
in precisely the sort of harsh landscapes that would later be of special
interest to early palaeontologists.

Even more than Hawkins, John Martin, who painted the frontispiece for *The Book of the Great Sea-dragons, Ichthyosauri and Plesiosauri*,
helped to disseminate the vision of Milton, in the emerging field
of palaeontology. Martin was already a phenomenally popular artist

who specialized in depicting biblical catastrophes. His paintings often showed very small human figures confronting the fury of the elements. For about a decade and a half before his collaboration with Hawkins, Martin had worked on an extensive set of engravings to illustrate Milton's *Paradise Lost*. They made heavy use of chiaroscuro to depict fantastic, tropical panoramas that were bathed in darkness and nearly desolate, except for a very few people. In the frontispiece, Martin extended this style to images of prehistoric creatures, showing them fighting and devouring one another on a dismal, moonlit shore. Martin also illustrated books by other early palaeontologists such as Gideon Mantell and popular writers with similar scenes of dinosaurs, pterosaurs and various sea creatures. With their bulging eyes, taut muscles and gaping jaws, they established the prevailing image of prehistoric life for a generation at least.

Milton's *Paradise Lost*, in brief, enabled people to visualize a world before the appearance of humankind. In nineteenth-century

John Martin, frontispiece to *The Book of the Great Sea-dragons, Ichthyosauri and Plesiosauri* (1840) by Thomas Hawkins. Early depictions of prehistoric creatures are often an exercise in Gothic horror.

John Martin, *Fallen Angels Entering Pandemonium*, 1841, illustration to Milton's *Paradise Lost*. Had this graphic been made a century or so later, it could easily have been taken for an illustration to some science fiction story about humans landing on a forbidding Martian landscape.

depictions, the pterosaur, a gigantic winged creature related to the dinosaurs, bore a special resemblance, with its bat-like wings, to demons of Western iconography. The early palaeontologist William Buckland and the novelist Charles Dickens both independently compared the creature to Milton's Satan.[8] Above all, *Paradise Lost* and just about all of the illustrations made to accompany it reflected a view of time and the cosmos as almost endlessly expansive. The horizons appear limitless, while even the most important figures are often very small.

When writers tried to combine the basic vision of Milton's *Paradise Lost* with recent palaeontological discoveries, the result was an epic narrative, including angels, demons, dinosaurs, mammoths, biblical prophets and so on. In her popular *Pre-Adamite Man* (1860), Isabella Duncan faulted Milton for overly generous use of poetic licence, and sought to correct his errors through a combination of palaeontology and scripture. Milton had claimed that God created humankind to replenish heaven after it had lost so many angels through Satan's rebellion. Duncan went further, arguing that the first of the two biblical creation narratives was not about Adam and Eve, but about a much earlier creation of human beings. The people in the first creation had eventually become angels or demons, depending on how they had lived. Drawing on contemporary research, she argued that pre-Adamite man and the animals of his time had been completely

John Martin, *The Country of the Iguanodon*, 1837. This watercolour was the frontispiece for Gideon Mantell's book *The Wonders of Geology* and applies conventions taken from Romantic and religious art to the depiction of prehistoric creatures.

destroyed by an ice age. Many stone axes and other tools had been found alongside the enormous bones of primeval creatures, but, Duncan argued, the lack of human bones from the same era showed that men and women had been transported to other realms.[9]

Paradise Lost had broken with many anthropocentric traditions, in that most of the characters had none of the usual human frailties and often only an approximation of human form. In another respect, however, *Paradise Lost* carried anthropocentrism to an almost unprecedented extreme, by centring much of the narrative around a human race that had not yet even been created. This set a precedent for many scientific books, both popular and professional, in centuries to come, which presented geology and evolution as part of a grand epic that would culminate in humankind.

Awe and wonder

The vast scale of deep time evoked religious awe, which blended with a sense of wonder at the intricate organization of natural forms. The study of the earth and its earlier inhabitants was not a matter of overcoming religious prejudice but, on the contrary, driven largely by religious passion. Until the late nineteenth century, particularly in Britain, a disproportionate number of the leading geologists and palaeontologists were clergy or at least highly religious laymen, among them Athanasius Kircher, Thomas Burnet, Robert Plot, Johann Jakob Scheuchzer, William Buckland, Georges Cuvier, Adam Sedgwick and William Conybeare. Even Charles Darwin, as a young man, considered a career in the ministry. Many of these figures, such as Scheuchzer and Buckland, began with the conscious intent of showing how science reinforced scripture or, as Milton famously put it in the opening lines of *Paradise Lost*, 'to justify God's ways to man', only to make discoveries that sabotaged their agenda.

In 1673, the prodigiously learned Jesuit Athanasius Kircher published *Arca Noë* (Noah's Ark), in which he used the great flood to explain many features of the modern world. The antediluvian era had been a time of giants, which explained the enormous bones that appeared from time to time. He also proposed an early theory of extinction by saying that some animals were not included in the ark. This idea went back to medieval iconography, where pictures of Noah's Ark, like other biblical scenes, had become in ways very conventionalized. Monkeys and other – for Europeans – exotic animals were seldom included. The unicorn was at times shown entering the ark, but dragons and griffins were not. Kircher partially explained this by saying that only pure varieties of animals had been saved. Accordingly, the giraffe or 'cameleopard' was not brought aboard, since it was a cross between a panther and a camel, while the armadillo was a hybrid of a hedgehog and a tortoise. Kircher also believed that dragons survived in caverns beneath the earth, which explained their appearance in stories such as that of St George.[10] Perhaps Kircher's greatest influence was dividing the story of the world into stages: antediluvian, postdiluvian and post-incarnation. This basic organization was used by many thinkers over the next few hundred years, and is still followed by many fundamentalists today.

In 1681, Thomas Burnet published his *Sacred Theory of the Earth*, in which he argued that the great flood, recorded in the biblical story of Noah, had completely transformed the earth. He argued first of all that the amount of water in the world, even including that condensed in the atmosphere, was not enough to entirely submerge all of the world's mountains. He concluded that water was contained below the surface of a hollow earth. To cleanse the world, God had intervened by temporarily opening the abyss, releasing the flood waters, then opened it again so the waters would subside after they had done their work. The flood was, in Burnet's words, 'a kind of dissolution of nature', when everything was transformed.[11] Not only were all people and animals destroyed, except for the few saved by Noah, but the surface of the globe, formerly completely regular, became deformed by mountains and valleys, and some irregularities filled entirely with water, creating rivers and seas. Prior to the flood, the axis of the earth had been completely vertical, and the climate always temperate. After the flood, the impact rendered the axis crooked, creating distinct seasons, while the irregularities created gales and storms. The earth also lost most of its primeval fertility, which had once enabled it to generate all forms of life, for it would not otherwise have been necessary for Noah to preserve the animals. Just as God had destroyed the old earth by water, the present one would eventually be consumed by fire, and yet another would be made in its place.

Though Burnet described the antediluvian world as a place of perfect order, harmony and symmetry, it became, as with Kircher before, a dumping ground for all anomalies, from ancient legends to dinosaur bones. The theories of Burnet and Kircher shared with Milton's poem a grandeur of scale and a cosmic drama which had few precedents in either scientific or literary writing. They did not think of the remote past as essentially timeless, but divided it into periods and filled it with stories. About a century later, researchers would also fill it with dinosaurs.

In the eighteenth century, the Swedish botanist Carl Linnaeus confronted a time, not entirely unlike ours, when a plethora of new discoveries and speculations seemed in danger of reducing the foundations of thought to chaos. New discoveries of both anthropoid apes and indigenous peoples, which were often confused with one another, moved early scientists to reconsider the very nature of humankind. Reports of strange creatures unlike any previously known to Europeans, such as the armadillo or the opossum, demonstrated that life might be more diverse than almost anybody had realized. On top of that, there were giant bones under the earth, and a huge range of creatures under the microscope. Linnaeus tried to banish this confusion by creating what may be the most elaborate order that any scientist has ever tried to superimpose on the bewildering diversity of living things. It involved placing all fauna and flora in a hierarchical system of classification with seven stages, corresponding to the biblical days of Creation. This made the strangest creatures seem almost familiar, and momentous changes seem illusory. Linnaeus saw himself as the new Adam, imposing order by naming the animals. The concept of a species was not formulated until Linnaeus published the first edition of his *Systema naturae* (1735), but, for many people, the fixity of species was very quickly assimilated into common sense. Yet geological investigations constantly uncovered fossil remains of animals and plants very unlike any that were known.

Closely associated with the idea of deep time was that of species extinction. Archaic cultures had seen biological identity as highly fluid, as shown by their frequent stories of transformations of people into animals and the reverse. The idea of species, considered as the ultimate unit in a hierarchical classification of living things, was not clearly articulated before Linnaeus, though it was partially implicit in the thought of the Middle Ages and Renaissance. Many artists had tried to make an inventory of all existing animals in illustrations of Noah's Ark, and a few authors, like Kircher, even attempted to diagram how they might all fit within the structure. Many people were profoundly troubled when Georges Cuvier proclaimed his theory of extinctions, also known as 'catastrophism', in his book *Essay on the Theory of the Earth* (French edition, 1813).

The sublime

The period in which dinosaurs were initially discovered was dominated by the Romantic movement, with its aesthetic of the sublime. That quality was contrasted with the beautiful, a neoclassical ideal that was based on harmonious proportions and restful contemplation. According to Edmund Burke in *A Philosophical Enquiry into the Origin of Our Ideas of the Sublime and Beautiful*, first published in 1757, the ultimate foundation of the sublime is terror. The feeling is evoked by grandness of scale. Bucolic landscapes with cultivated gardens might be beautiful, but harsh, forbidding ones were sublime.[12]

To a great extent, the discovery of deep time was also part of the Romantic reaction to the modern world. The rapid pace of industrialization generated nostalgia for the distant past, which seemed more natural and authentic. As the destruction of rural landscapes progressed, the reaction became more extreme. The bucolic meditations of poets like Wordsworth and Keats were no longer in fashion. Writers such as Tennyson, illustrators such as Doré and painters such as Turner and Delacroix showed an epic conflict between nature and humankind. More pastoral visions seemed to be disproved by reports that explorers constantly brought back, of primeval woods filled with monstrous snakes and cannibals. The dinosaurs would epitomize all of the fear and fascination of primeval times.

Above all, Romantic artists and poets saw the sublime in irregular geological formations such as the moors of Scotland and, most especially, the mountains of Switzerland. These were celebrated by poets such as Byron and Tennyson. They were the setting for influential works of literature such as *Frankenstein* by Mary Shelley, *Wuthering Heights* by Emily Brontë and *The Bride of Lammermoor* by Walter Scott, as well as countless popular Gothic novels. For well over a century, poets constantly wavered between the idea of the beautiful, which comprised social duties, and that of the sublime, which entailed personal isolation. The landscapes that people considered transcendent were, not so coincidentally, the ones that preoccupied early geologists such as James Hutton and Charles Lyell, as well as palaeontologists such as Cuvier. The opening of vast expanses of time inspired awe. Deep time was a sublime realm, and the dinosaurs became its gods. For the many who felt frustrated by the pettiness of modern, bourgeois existence, they seemed to exemplify life on an epic scale.

According to Daniel Worster,

That the Galápagos or the Andes might provide certain pleasures to Darwin precisely because they were savage and terrifying was a consequence of the emotional tutoring he and others of his generation had received. By the 1830s it had become a common impulse on both sides of the Atlantic to seek out especially those natural experiences that left fear in the heart.[13]

The scientists of the era, like the poets, sought to become one with the natural world, through confrontation with its violence and savagery. This intensity of nature was, of course, manifested in tempests, earthquakes, deluges and volcanoes, all of which also figured prominently in the world of early geologists and palaeontologists. On a more daily basis, its most important manifestations were predation and other conflicts among animals. In the perspective of deep time, its dramatic manifestation was species extinction, which was proclaimed in the writings of Georges Cuvier. And the image that best summed up all of these themes would be a predatory dinosaur fighting with its intended prey, perhaps beneath a red sky with volcanoes in the background.

Finally, in 1859 Darwin's *On the Origin of Species* provided a concept of 'struggle for existence' that could bring high drama to events in deep time. It consisted of competition among species, biological families and so on. These, in turn, might be used as surrogates for human beings, either individually or collectively. If a megalosaurus fought an iguanodon, one might pick a champion to cheer for. And groups like crocodilians, amphibians, dinosaurs and mammals were like nations vying for supremacy.

Milton had pioneered a way of depicting prehistoric times, with harsh landscapes, expansive horizons, deathly conflicts, mighty figures and intense but simple emotions. This is still followed in visual art featuring dinosaurs today. It is a world in which everything takes on epic proportions, where everything is dangerous but nothing is trivial, and it offers us an escape from the mundane details of everyday life.

Illustration showing the entrance to Hell, from the Hours of Catherine of Cleves,
c. 1440. In medieval times the netherworld was often depicted as an enormous mouth
in which sinners were devoured.

CHAPTER III

Mister Big and Mister Fierce

I would give ten years off the beginning of my life to see, only once,
Tyrannosaurus rex come rearing up from the elms of Central Park, a Morgan
police horse screaming in its jaws. We can never have enough of nature.
EDWARD ABBEY, *Down the River*

Hell in many cultures is traditionally depicted as a wide-open mouth with sharp teeth. To become prey is a common metaphor for death. Predation is also a metaphor for life, since we live by consuming other living things. But predation provides another, more positive, metaphor through the thrill of the chase, and life has, in consequence, often been conceived as a quest. The cultural anthropologist Walter Burkert has even argued, in *Creation of the Sacred* (1996), that storytelling, and thereby human culture, goes back to the chase. Hunting and being threatened by predators were certainly almost universal experiences of early human beings, and they can easily evoke intense emotion today.

Herders and agriculturalists view animals in ways that are fundamentally opposed. For herders, predators are a continuous threat to their livelihood. For agriculturalists, predators are a blessing, since they kill the animals that devour their crops. This rivalry between the two groups is a foundation for the biblical story of the first murder, when Cain, a farmer, kills Abel, a shepherd. The opposition is complicated by the alliance of human beings with dogs, which are predators but learn to defend sheep. But the basic attitudes have continued throughout history, and both herd animals and predators are still regarded with great ambivalence. For the most part, rulers and aristocratic families, which obtained wealth from their lands, have identified with carnivorous animals such as wolves, bears and lions. Peasants, who looked after farm animals and perhaps longed for a more egalitarian order, have felt closer to herbivorous animals such as cattle and sheep.

Alongside nostalgic images of an Edenic past is a counter-myth in which life begins in unceasing violence and predation. The earth was once the domain of monstrous, usually reptilian, predators that would constantly devour almost anything they encountered. These monsters include the Egyptian Apophis, the Mesopotamian children of Tiamat, the Greek Titans and the Zoroastrian creations of Ahriman. In Greek mythology, for example, Uranus would eat his children, as many predators often do, as soon as they were born. His partner Gaia rescued one of the children, Cronos, who then overthrew Uranus, but also ate his own offspring. These myths express a perspective in which the world, largely through the efforts of gods and heroes, becomes gradually more civilized, yet retains a foundation of primeval violence, which might erupt at any time and plunge the world back into chaos.

Many Abrahamic traditions tied the original sin of men and women to the carnivorous activity among animals. In the original tale of Eden, all animals had once been peaceful and domestic. They not only refrained from eating one another but also spoke like human beings, which is why it did not seem strange when the serpent first addressed Eve. By many traditions, animals had not preyed upon one another until after they were saved from the flood by Noah, and God announced his New Covenant with humankind. Otherwise, they would have eaten one another in the ark. The prophet Isaiah

Boy seated in the mouth of a model *Tyranosaurus rex* in Park Wroclawski, Lubin, Poland. Our fascination with dinosaurs has always centred largely on predation, and even becoming prey can have a paradoxical appeal.

had predicted a reconciliation of carnivorous animals and their prey: 'The wolf and the young lamb will feed together, the lion eat straw like an ox ... They will do no hurt, no harm on all my holy mountain' (65:25, Jerusalem Bible). In medieval Christianity, Hell was generally thought of as a place of constant predation, in which demons forever cook, devour and eliminate sinners.

With the emergence of modern geology and the discovery of dinosaurs in the eighteenth and nineteenth centuries, people at first imagined primeval times as an era of chaotic and unceasing violence, in which monstrous creatures perpetually fought with and then consumed one another. The aeons that followed were a gradual 'civilizing' process that culminated in modern European society. Though some dinosaurs such as the iguanodon were modelled after herbivores, even they were frequently depicted baring large, sharp teeth, and in threatening poses. With the advent of Darwin's theory of evolution, simply surviving came to be seen as a form of predation, since it could be done only at the expense of other, competing creatures.

For Western people of the nineteenth century, particularly the British, the reason why some animals eat others was not simply a scientific problem but also a metaphysical one. The study of nature was still largely inspired by natural theology, which sought to reveal the divine plan in the natural world and prove the wisdom of God. From this point of view, even the existence of flesh eaters came across as an apparent defect in the very nature of the cosmos, a manifestation of cruelty in the foundation of the universe. The defining text of the school was the book *Natural Theology* by William Paley, who wrote that 'the subject ... of animals *devouring* one another, forms the chief, if not the only instance, in the works of the Deity, of an economy stamped by marks of design, in which the character of utility can be called in question.'[1] He discussed the problem at considerable length, arguing that death was necessary, since the world could not support an endless number of creatures. The great fertility of certain species such as herrings or minnows requires that predatory species keep their numbers in check, so they do not completely overrun the world. Finally, death by a predator was relatively merciful in comparison to alternatives such as a slow demise from disease or starvation.

These considerations were certainly consistent with Paley's main argument that all features of the natural world were synchronized so that all life would prosper, something he saw as proof of the wisdom and benevolence of God. The contention was reasonable to a point, but it was emotionally unsatisfying when one contemplated the extent of suffering in the world. Even Paley was not entirely pleased with it, and this added a slightly melancholy note to his usual tone, which moved between enthusiasm and analytic detachment. He confessed he could not entirely resolve the problem, stating that 'it is probable that many more reasons belong than those of which we are in possession.'[2] William Smellie, the first editor of *Encyclopædia Britannica*, expressed his anguish far more directly, observing that, 'Through almost the whole of nature . . . nothing but rapine and destruction of individuals prevail.' He offered arguments similar to Paley's that the destruction of some creatures might lead to the greater good of others, yet he still felt compelled to ask, 'Why has Nature established a system so cruel? Why did she render it necessary that one animal could not live without the destruction of another?' He then confessed his helplessness before this mystery, saying, 'To such questions no answer can be given or expected. No being except the Supreme can unfold this mystery.'[3]

In the nineteenth century, many people viewed predators such as the tiger essentially as demons, even if the scorn was often mixed with admiration for their beauty. Wolves were hunted to extinction in much of Europe and almost exterminated in the United States. The campaign to rid the world of large predators, particularly those that killed livestock, became a moral crusade. The sea of ichthyosaurs and plesiosaurs was initially understood as one of absolutely unrestrained predation, of 'eat and be eaten'. The primeval monsters in pictures of the early nineteenth century are always literally at one another's throats, to a point where one must wonder how any could have ever reached maturity. As it happened, dinosaurs were discovered in approximately the same historic era when belief in dragons, devils and angels began to fade. Inevitably, dinosaurs stepped into the vacancy they had left, acquiring the symbolism from all three predecessors.

Megalosaurus and iguanodon

We think of dinosaurs in terms of an archetypal pair, a fierce carnivore and a huge, formidable herbivore. This pattern goes back to the initial two dinosaurs, which were discovered at about the same time in England around the start of the 1820s. *Megalosaurus*, a predator related to *Tyrannosaurus rex*, was first named by William Buckland in 1824, and *Iguanodon*, an enormous herbivore, was named about two years later by Gideon Mantell. Over the next several decades, they were constantly mentioned and depicted side by side, together creating the public image of dinosaurs.

The megalosaurus bones found by Buckland in Oxfordshire were, like all the early finds of dinosaurs, fragmentary, but Buckland determined on the basis of the lower jaw that it was reptilian and carnivorous. He conceptualized it as a giant monitor lizard. Cuvier had, on the basis of such a comparison, estimated that it was about 12 metres (40 ft) long. William Conybeare, a friend of Buckland, described it in a lecture as follows:

> To the head of the lizard, it united the teeth of a crocodile,
> a neck of enormous length, resembling the body of a serpent,
> a trunk and tail having proportions of an ordinary quadruped,
> the ribs of a chameleon, and the paddles of a whale.[4]

But nobody really knew how to visualize such a creature, and popular publications conventionalized their images for easy recognition.

Though the first dinosaur ever to be named, the megalosaurus did not make the sort of immediate sensation that we might perhaps have expected. One reason is that precisely the novelty of a giant, prehistoric lizard made the idea difficult for people to absorb. Another reason why news of the discovery did not create an immediate sensation is that communications at the time were much slower than they would become later in the nineteenth century, to say nothing of the present. The first railways had just been built, but they were still experimental and not extensive. Printing was still a relatively laborious process. Another reason is that the idea of a giant predator as the sole ruler of the planet, without even a credible adversary, would have been distressing, and could even have suggested the Devil himself.

But the megalosaurus had a formidable adversary in waiting. At the time, people generally imagined new animals as differing only in scale from those that were alive at present. A giant tooth was found by fossil hunter Mary Ann Mantell, who presented it to her husband, Gideon Mantell. He determined that the tooth closely resembled that of an iguana, though on a vastly larger scale. Associated with it was a thigh bone, more than twice the width of one that had once belonged to megalosaurus. Gideon Mantell named the creature *Iguanodon*, meaning 'iguana tooth'. Extrapolating from the ratio of tooth size and length in an iguana, he initially estimated that the lizard was about 30.5 metres (100 ft) long.[5] Observing that some iguanas have horns, Mantell placed a claw from the foot on the nose of the iguanodon, making it look a bit like a rhinoceros.

Iguanodon and megalosaurus were used to express, in a very monumental way, what was perhaps the dominant theme running through Victorian culture: the conflict between savagery and civilization. The battles among ichthyosaurs and plesiosaurs, drawn by artists such as John Martin, simply rendered the ubiquitous violence of early life. The two were usually shown in a ferocious battle or with one

Illustration to *Gately's World's Progress: A General History of the Earth's Construction and of the Advancement of Mankind* (1865), edited by C. E. Beale, showing an iguanodon fighting a megalosaurus. A few decades earlier, Gideon Mantell had identified the iguanodon as a herbivore by an examination of its tooth. Much of the public, however, thought of deep time as a sort of carnivorous free-for-all.

devouring the other's corpse. The conflicts of the megalosaurus and iguanodon were a bit subtler. At times, as in *The Country of the Iguanodon*, John Martin's frontispiece to Gideon Mantell's book *Wonders of Geology* (1838), they are indeed locked in life-and-death combat. An iguanodon has apparently triumphed over one megalosaurus and is crushing it, but another megalosaurus has attacked it from behind.

More often, the two dinosaurs are in fairly close proximity, but there is only a suggestion of potential conflict. Typical is the frontispiece for the book *Sketches in Prose and Verse* by George Richardson (1838), drawn by George Nibbs, which shows an iguanodon prominently in the foreground. It gazes at a pair of ichthyosaurs with a big smile. In the shadowy background, a megalosaurus looks on with a posture that seems threatening but impotent. The message is that the peaceful

A megalosaurus fighting an iguanodon, from J. W. Buel, *Sea and Land* (1897). Prehistoric creatures gave Victorian artists an excuse to indulge relatively freely in a taste for images of unrestrained bloodlust and terror, akin to late medieval depictions of Hell or modern horror movies.

Frontispiece by Fernand Besnier to *Le Monde avant la création de l'homme* (1886) by Camille Flammarion. Many books represented the Mesozoic era as one of unrestrained violence and predation. Here all animals, even the vegetarian iguanodon, seem poised to tear one another to pieces.

iguanodon is king of this domain, and many carnivorous animals would like to challenge it but cannot. As Richardson wrote in reference to an illustration that introduced readers to Gideon Mantell's collection of fossils, 'the colossal iguanodon . . . appears to reign undisputed monarch of the wild and wondrous scene.'[6] The iguanodon was a bit like the British Empire ruling exotic kingdoms in remote parts of the globe. Eventually, a few scenes from deep time even began to take on a bucolic ambience, reflecting the Victorian idealization of family life. In an illustration to Franz Unger's book *The Primitive World* (1851), a family of iguanodons in a luxurious rainforest is so secure that it can engage in recreation. Two juvenile iguanodons confront one another playfully, a bit like puppies, across the back of their mother.[7]

The Crystal Palace sculptures displayed in London in 1854 first brought dinosaurs to widespread public attention, and in the centre of the display were two iguanodons and a megalosaurus. Like other public exhibits of dinosaurs up to the present, they had to maintain a delicate balance between the goals of entertainment and education. Storytelling was not permitted, or at least was kept to a minimum. To avoid any hint of sensationalism, the animals were kept in rather heraldic poses, and seem to relate to one another very little. The megalosaurus gazes from a distance at one of the iguanodons, crouching like a tiger. The iguanodon serenely looks away, knowing that it is ready for any challenge. The potential for violence is hinted at, but no conflict is shown. Part of the reason was to avoid appearing threatening to the public, especially to children. Contemporary cartoons suggest that the models scared people, though only in an amusement-park sort of way. The models provided a relief from the unceasing violence that people like Thomas Hawkins and John Martin had

George Nibbs, frontispiece for the book *Sketches in Prose and Verse* (1838) by George Richardson. The iguanodon here can afford to be genial, since no creature can challenge its dominion.

Print showing the Crystal Palace dinosaurs, London, *c.* 1860. Perhaps to soften their appearance of ferocity, the model dinosaurs are placed in an extremely cultivated landscape.

depicted in the prehistoric world. Nevertheless, the isolation could make the creatures seem a bit stiff and lethargic.

Tyrannosaurus and triceratops

Dinosaurs – and, obliquely, humankind – are now often represented in the popular imagination primarily by the *Tyrannosaurus rex*, whose image is widely disseminated. Today, when an Internet connection fails, the computer screen will often show a picture of a slightly melancholy tyrannosaurus, together with a note of apology. David Hone writes, 'Perhaps no scientific name is as well-known as *Tyrannosaurus rex* . . .

and the animal that bears that name is easily the most popular and best-known dinosaur with the general public.'[8] This is an exaggeration, but a very common one, which can tell us a bit about ourselves. Other dinosaurs have been mentioned and depicted about as often as tyrannosaurus, but none evokes the same combination of horror and identification. We human beings are probably trying to project at least some of the guilt we feel for our destruction of the natural world onto another creature. We may also feel an impulse to posthumously domesticate the ferocious monster, much as our ancestors once did with the wolf, something suggested by the proliferation of cuddly tyrannosaurs as toys for children.

Triceratops was discovered in 1887 and named by Othniel Marsh the next year. A few bones of *Tyrannosaurus rex* were first discovered in the 1890s, and the dinosaur was not named until 1905. The popularity of the pair took off just as that of megalosaurus and iguanodon started to fade. We are looking here at four dinosaurs, but two archetypes – Mister Fierce and Mister Big. The former is a giant predator with huge jaws, sharp teeth and formidable claws. The latter is an enormous

A model ichthyosaurus in Crystal Palace Park, London. It is hard to know how much the effect was intentional, but when the water level is high this figure will seem fully aquatic, with only the snout and part of the back protruding from the water. When the water is low, it can seem almost fully terrestrial.

herbivore, which may be gifted formidable weapons yet might also use its bulk for purposes of defence. Unlike their predecessors megalosaurus and iguanodon, tyrannosaurus and triceratops were just about evenly matched, or at least that was how images in mass media made them seem. A set of conventions for depicting the pair developed very quickly. They were usually shown facing off against one another, but not yet fighting, almost as though they were frozen in time, with no indication of which, if either, would be the eventual victor. One exception is in Disney's film *Fantasia* (1940), where the tyrannosaurus is victorious but quickly succumbs to a natural disaster.

The murals of dinosaurs painted in the late nineteenth to midtwentieth centuries by Charles R. Knight for the Field Museum in Chicago and the American Museum of Natural History in New York

Painting by Charles R. Knight showing a brontosaurus in the water and a diplodocus on land, 1897. This painting, done in an Impressionist style, became the model for countless subsequent depictions of both dinosaurs.

Early photograph showing the dinosaur models created by Benjamin Waterhouse Hawkins, from *The Primitive World* by Franz Unger (1859 edition). The raised head of the iguanodon indicates its dominance over the other dinosaurs.

did more to establish the public perception of dinosaurs than any other works since the sculptures of Benjamin Waterhouse Hawkins for the Crystal Palace Park. They shared the same monumental scale, combined spectacle with pedagogy and addressed the tension between these aspirations in much the same way. A scene of carnage would probably have appealed to the public, and it would certainly have been in line with the idea of dinosaurs as an embodiment of primitive bestiality. It would not, however, have been appropriate in displays intended largely for children.

Knight's mural of *Tyrannosaurus rex* facing off against triceratops, which Knight produced for the Field Museum in the early 1920s, is still one of the most iconic representations of dinosaurs ever created. Like Waterhouse Hawkins before him, Knight chose to suggest violence without actually showing it. There is actually no evidence that these two giants ever engaged in combat. It seems unlikely that even tyrannosaurus would have taken on such a formidable adversary unless the triceratops was obviously enfeebled by illness, disease or age. In Knight's mural, they are gazing at one another across a considerable distance, perhaps sizing one another up. There is enough hint of a confrontation to add excitement, yet nothing to offend either scientific or emotional sensibilities. The result is a moment fixed in time, a bit like a posed photograph.

Murals that were similar in style were often produced for major centres of government and commerce during the same period, showing larger-than-life figures from history and mythology. They were especially popular among communists and fascists, but also common in the United States and Britain. They expressed the vast ambitions that were shared by advocates of all ideologies, including Bolshevism and American capitalism. From the metro in Moscow to the Rockefeller Center in New York, it was an era infatuated with bigness, but only dinosaurs could be painted in such a grand manner without rhetorical exaggeration. The tyrannosaurus and triceratops gazing at one another from a distance suggested the tense, uneasy peace among heavily armed superpowers.

Allosaurus and barosaurus

In the vestibule at the main entrance to the American Museum of Natural History is a group of mounted dinosaur skeletons in a dramatic confrontation of predator and prey. A barosaurus, a willowy relative of apatosaurus, is rearing up to a gigantic height on its hind legs. In front of it is an allosaurus, an earlier relative of tyrannosaurus, and a juvenile barosaurus is peeking out over the giant's tail. The larger barosaurus is the mother of the smaller one, and she is trying to crush the allosaurus beneath her forelegs, but the adversary is endeavouring to circle around behind her and grab the baby. Which dinosaur will succeed?

Which of these 4 dinosaurs is your favorite?

(See them in Sinclair Dinoland at the World's Fair)

BRONTOSAURUS, a 70-foot dinosaur . . . roamed the earth over a hundred million years ago when Nature was mellowing the petroleum that Sinclair now refines into the best gasolines and oils.

TRICERATOPS means "three horns on the face." This 10-ton dinosaur lived in Montana and Wyoming during the Cretaceous Period.

ANKYLOSAURUS looks dangerous but this 20-foot "walking fortress" was a harmless vegetarian.

TYRANNOSAURUS, largest, fiercest meat-eater that ever lived. He had teeth 6 inches long—and a mouth as big as a power shovel.

We know *our* favorite. It's *Brontosaurus* . . . Sinclair's famous trademark. Millions saw him and 8 other life-sized dinosaurs in Sinclair Dinoland at the New York World's Fair. We hope you and your family come to the Fair this summer . . . See this exciting re-creation of prehistoric times.

For a more pleasant trip, we'll be happy to plan your route through interesting sections of the country. For example, the *Dixieland Trail* covers

5 southern states, takes you over 6000-foot peaks to secluded ocean beaches, historic forts, battlegrounds, elegant antebellum homes, many other landmarks of the old South.

This Sinclair service is free. Write Sinclair Tour Bureau, 600 Fifth Avenue, New York, N. Y. 10020. Tell us the areas you want to visit in U. S., Canada or Mexico.

Sinclair

Advertisement for Sinclair Oil's Dinoland pavilion at the 1964 World's Fair in New York. Themes and motifs from Charles R. Knight's dinosaur paintings were widely copied. In this picture, the tyrannosaurus and triceratops face one another menacingly without actually fighting, just as in Knight's mural in Chicago's Field Museum.

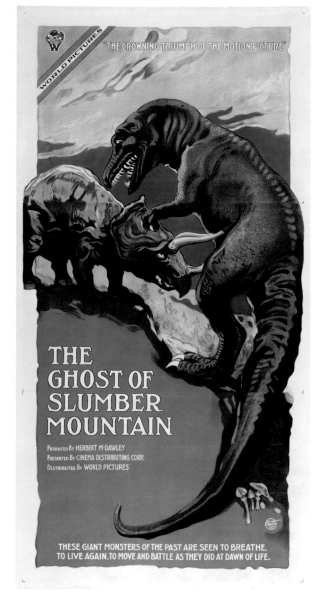

Poster advertising the film *The Ghost of Slumber Mountain* (1918), produced by Herbert M. Dawley and with special effects by Willis O'Brien. The poster is more graphic than most others of the period and shows a battle of the titans that artists tended only to hint at. The film pioneered techniques of stop-motion photography, which enabled films to combine real actors and animated creatures on the screen, opening the way for many more films about dinosaurs over the next century.

RESTORATION OF THE TRICERATOPS AND TYRANNOSAURUS

Postcard of c. 1930 from the Field Museum in Chicago, based on a detail of the mural by Charles R. Knight, showing tyrannosaurus facing off against triceratops. The way the two giants eye one another warily suggests the tension among the great powers as the Second World War approached.

John Margolies, tyrannosaurus and triceratops, Dinosaur Park, Rapid City, South Dakota. The dinosaurs have become so familiar that they seem a bit like the characters from Disney cartoons, and the combat of giants has become an occasion for 'wholesome family fun'.

Unlike the confrontations between tyrannosaurus and triceratops, this one will be decided less by strategy than by brute force. Like them, it may not actually lead to violence. There is enough suspense to be exciting, but the mama seems to have the upper hand, in regard to size, manoeuvrability and even position.

Around the three dinosaurs is the usual palatial splendour, with a dome modelled on that of the Pantheon, an ancient temple in Rome. The ceiling is supported by granite Corinthian columns, and the floor is marble. On the wall are mural scenes taken largely from the life of Theodore Roosevelt, a major patron of the museum. Our eyes are drawn upwards along the curved spine from the back to the head of the mother barosaurus.

The scaffolding that holds plaster casts of the original skeletons in place is a very impressive example of the blacksmith's craft. Beyond that, what is one to call it? It is not, in any conventional sense, very scientific. The American Museum openly admits that there is no objective evidence that such scenes ever took place.[9] The barosaurus would have had to pivot and land with great speed and agility to have had even a chance of crushing a running allosaurus. A sign accompanying the exhibit states that the barosaurus must at least have been able to rear up on its hind legs, since it could not have mated in any other way, but this is only partly true. Only the male would probably have needed to rear up, and not as high as the model skeleton, but the dinosaur here is presented as a female. Scientist Stephen J. Gould has stated that 'most of my colleagues would consider such a posture ridiculously unlikely.'[10]

In many ways, the display seems closer to art than to science, so why is it in a natural history museum rather than an art gallery? But perhaps the two activities have never been as distinct as most people used to think. Both art and science blend reason with imagination, however much their emphasis may differ. The display dates from the early 1990s, and it openly indulges in the sort of storytelling that professional decorum had previously not allowed. Science has shed

The mounted skeleton of the barosaurus at the American Museum of Natural History, shown rearing up dramatically as if to defend her baby.

much of its old formality, so stylistic flourishes are now permitted in displays as well as even in journal articles.

One figure here, the allosaurus, is notable for its ferocity, the other, here the barosaurus, for its size. The first is essentially a barbarian, and the other a defender of domestic – that is, 'civilized' – life. All in all, the pose of the three dinosaurs seems artificial, and more like a dance than a realistic scene. It is a bit like the dance of death, as depicted in medieval and early modern paintings, with human skeletons grasping one another and frolicking together. An even better analogy would be the dioramas made for the Mexican Day of the Dead, in which skeletons are shown engaged in all the activities of people in everyday life, from working in an office to preparing dinner. There is something a bit ironic in such a drama, enacted by figures so long, and so obviously, deceased. Perhaps what it shows is how dinosaurs often seem to us at once completely dead and yet very much alive.

Dinosaur blood

Educational materials on dinosaurs used to be remarkably discreet about predation. It was a bit like sex in a lot of old comedies – constantly hinted at and referred to yet never shown. The predators and herbivores would eye one another warily, and it often appeared as if one was going to attack, yet we might never see even a drop of dinosaur blood. The necessity for suggesting violence indirectly adds subtlety to works like the murals of Charles R. Knight, though it can also make the dinosaurs seem oddly static and restrained. This even carries over into old movies such as *Godzilla*, where the monster ravages an entire city in a rather fastidious way, doing far more damage to structures than to human beings.

That decorum crumbles quickly in the Jurassic Park novels of Michael Crichton, as well as in the blockbuster movies that have been made of them, which make up a veritable orgy of violence. The first novel, *Jurassic Park* (1990), tells of an attempt to clone dinosaurs for a theme park on an island near Costa Rica. The monsters escape, though scientists and technicians try in vain to contain them. At last, the Costa Rican air force bombs the island, but not until several have escaped into the Amazon. The sequel, *The Lost World* (1995), is set four years later, as the theme park is being established on a neighbouring island. A group of mercenaries, hunters and palaeontologists comes to capture dinosaurs for a new theme park to be set up in San Diego. To prevent that, people who work at Jurassic Park let several dinosaurs out of their cages, after which they wreak havoc for a while. A *Tyrannosaurus rex* actually is captured and brought to San Diego, where it escapes and starts to destroy the city, before it is finally lured back to a ship and returned. I will not go into details of the plots, for they are no more than an excuse to string together a series of fast-paced chase scenes, in which dinosaurs terrify children, turn over cars, make people scream, knock down buildings and devour human beings. Each of the two novels was the basis for a blockbuster film directed by Steven Spielberg, which are both among the highest-grossing movies of all time. They were followed by two other Jurassic Park movies, which, though not based on books by Crichton or directed by Spielberg, were also blockbusters, and the franchise may be just getting started.

The author listed some distinguished palaeontologists as consultants to his novels including John Ostrom, Robert Bakker and Jack Horner, which may seem to give the books status among educators, but, while careful about a few details, the books do not let science get in the way of entertainment. They make the dinosaur velociraptor the size of a large man and as smart as a chimpanzee, when it was really the size of a turkey and probably less bright. Furthermore, even though the park is supposedly about the Jurassic period, most of the dinosaurs belong to the Cretaceous. The novels insert a lot of scientific theories through dialogue and make heavy use of Robert Bakker's claim that dinosaurs were warm-blooded. Accordingly, dinosaurs are shown as active, quick and needing plenty of prey to maintain their metabolism.

While this sounds progressive, it is largely a rationalization for a stereotype of dinosaurs that goes back to Victorian times. In fact, the movies, like early painters such as John Martin, take this idea to an extreme. Even large predators such as lions will rest and may go for several days without food after feasting on a major kill, but the cinematic dinosaurs appear completely insatiable. As David Gilmore has put it, the *Tyrannosaurus rex* in *Jurassic Park* 'is little more than a walking mouth with dagger-like teeth'.[11]

One of the main characters in *Jurassic Park*, the mathematician Ian Malcolm, who seems to be a spokesman for Crichton himself, constantly invokes chaos theory, arguing essentially that when you try to manage too many things, some of them are sure to go wrong. This sounds very modern or even postmodern, but it is very much in the spirit of the Victorians, who were also obsessed with chaos (or 'savagery') and order (or 'civilization'), a dichotomy that has lived on in many thrillers over the past century and more. Essentially, the novels and the movies based on them return to the view of dinosaurs expressed by writers like Thomas Hawkins and artists like John Martin, as creatures that do nothing but hunt and eat one another. The entertainments also exploit the traditional iconography of demons and monsters to make the world of dinosaurs into the setting for what are, in most respects, fairly conventional horror movies.

The dinosaurs in both the books and the films are essentially the 'living dead' – in other words, zombies. They have been artificially restored to life, and belong to neither nature nor society. This is particularly true of the velociraptors, which, like cinematic zombies, hunt in packs and attack relentlessly. The tyrannosaurus, by contrast, can be an agent of divine justice like Godzilla in earlier films, who saves decent people from other monsters. At the end of the first movie, the tyrant lizard rescues the terrified scientists and their companions by killing a pack of velociraptors. In *The Lost World*, the human villain of the story is carried away by a mother tyrannosaurus to her nest, where he is fed to her babies, and the author describes

Scene from the movie *Jurassic Park* (1993) showing a *Tyrannosaurus rex* attacking a truck. Our fantasies about dinosaurs have not changed a great deal since they were first discovered in the early 19th century.

his demise in very graphic detail. It is the Devil carrying a sinner to Hell, where he will, as in many paintings from the late Middle Ages and Renaissance, be eaten and excreted by demons. One might even interpret the ravages of tyrannosaurus in places like San Diego as a punishment for, or warning against, the hubris of mankind.

Since the Jurassic Park books and movies, popular culture has focused heavily on predatory dinosaurs. In the words of Alan A. Debus, 'Now raptors are veritable monsters not only due to their inherent savagery, but also for their crafty, menacing intellect.'[12] It is hard to say whether they inspire horror more by attacking us or by resembling us. But, if deinonychus, velociraptor and their relatives appear human-like, the great sauropods remain embodiments of fate, lingering quietly in the background and invulnerable to any challenge.

Artists such as Waterhouse Hawkins and Knight found ways to present predation with discretion, constantly hinting at, yet not quite showing, extreme violence. If Mister Fierce was scary, Mister Big would be on hand to reassure us. He distracted the monster away from people and, by his imposing presence, forced it to behave. But it was probably inevitable that the delicate restraints which enabled us to contemplate dinosaurs with equanimity would break down eventually, allowing us to indulge in an orgy of terror, guilt, righteousness and triumph. Killing, predation and blood are now common in representations of dinosaurs, even ones intended for young people. After crouching and glaring for over a century and a half, megalosaurus has finally pounced.

Predator or prey?

What is the most popular dinosaur ever? There is now a fairly objective way to measure this: a device from Google called the Ngram Viewer, which totals up the percentage of books that mention a certain word from the year 1800 to 2000. On 20 March 2017, I went to the website that hosts this device and typed in the names of various dinosaurs to compare how often they came up in literature.[13] The dinosaur most mentioned by a huge margin was the iguanodon, whose fame peaks in the year 1851. This apex of popular attention is more than five times greater than the peak of the tyrannosaurus, which comes in the year 1997.

By 1860, the popularity of iguanodon had declined by about two-thirds, though it still remained easily the most popular dinosaur until about the middle of the first decade of the twentieth century, when it was rivalled and eventually surpassed by others including tyrannosaurus, triceratops and diplodocus. Those three dinosaurs, however, are primarily American, and owe much of their popularity to the ways they have been used to embody an image of North America as 'the New Eden', an unspoiled land of primordial vitality. When, however, the search is done of only books in British English, the iguanodon, despite many ups and downs, was still the most popular dinosaur as we entered the twenty-first century.

When we compare the relative popularity of iguanodon and megalosaurus over the decades, it is remarkable that the mention of the two dinosaurs rises and falls in almost exactly the same curve, though iguanodon remains consistently a bit higher. The same basic pattern applies to the other dinosaurs that are frequently paired such as tyrannosaurus and triceratops. The public took little notice of either dinosaur until 1916, when the popularity of *Tyrannosaurus rex* suddenly shot up, and that of triceratops followed. For most of the next century, they were close to being equal in popularity, with tyrannosaurus usually, though by no means always, a bit ahead. This strongly indicates that the two dinosaurs were usually, or at least very often, mentioned together as a pair.

This curve, I believe, tells us a great deal, about our attitudes not only towards dinosaurs but, more broadly, towards carnivores and herbivores in general. People are thrilled by the primeval fierceness of large predators such as tyrannosaurs, eagles and tigers, which evoke a combination of identification and fear. To indulge freely in our impulse to admire them, we must first be reassured that they can be subdued, or at least seriously challenged, whether that is by human hunters or by an adversary such as the iguanodon.

The phenomenal commercial success of the Jurassic Park novels and movies shows that they tapped into something that had probably always been present just beneath the surface in the study and representation of dinosaurs: a fascination with unrestrained appetite and power. It is the ability that predators from tigers to pythons still possess to transfix us in a combination of fear and admiration. The existence of predation in nature is as difficult to accept as ever, and people today still constantly waver between the glorification and extermination of carnivorous animals.

Though we now intellectually recognize the ecological importance of predation far more clearly than the Victorians did, we remain as ambivalent about it as they. The Victorians openly spoke of predation as 'savagery', and our language is more euphemistic, but our attitudes are much the same as theirs. We still move between extremes of demonization and idealization in our attitudes towards predators from tyrannosaurus to the grey wolf. Paul Trout has identified 'the most primal human fear' as that of 'being ripped apart and eaten alive by an animal'.[14] Over the millennia, we have negotiated with, worshipped, fought and often exterminated large predators. We have also become perhaps the deadliest predator of all, but that terror is still with us. We think of life in primeval times as reduced to its barest essentials, and our simplest, most vivid image of that era is of two giants, a meat-eater and an herbivore, locked in mortal combat.

The skull of Sue the *Tyrannosaurus rex* at the Field Museum in Chicago. The museum purchased the skeleton, the largest and most complete of a tyrannosaurus ever found, in 1997 for $7.6 million, with the sponsorship of McDonald's. The record price reflects a growing fascination with *T. rex* and other large predators.

CHAPTER IV

From the Crystal Palace to Jurassic Park

I don't care a straw for your newspaper articles; my constituents don't know
how to read, but they can't help seeing them damned pictures.
WILLIAM 'BOSS' TWEED

Modern museums grew out of the 'curiosity cabinets' kept mostly by eccentric rulers and aristocrats. These, in turn, were often inspired by a macabre fascination with novelty, as well as by piety and a rather mundane inquisitiveness. Cabinets of curiosity contained anything that attracted attention, from shrunken human heads purchased from Latin American tribes to feathers from birds of paradise in New Guinea. They contained stuffed bodies and skeletons of exotic animals. These were occasionally mixed in with those of fantastic creatures such as dragons, stitched together from the parts of many animals and sold to gullible collectors. There were also many shells, coins, colourful rocks and fossils. Like hoarders of today, the keepers of cabinets of curiosity indulged freely in their eccentricities.

Collecting cabinets of curiosity grew in part out of reliquaries, and they first became popular in the Renaissance. Perhaps the most avid collector of all was the Holy Roman Emperor Rudolf II, in the early seventeenth century, who, alongside a vast collection of bezoars

Ole Worm's cabinet of curiosities, frontispiece to *Museum Wormianum* (Copenhagen, 1655). The old curiosity cabinets were unabashedly idiosyncratic and included just about anything that appealed to the owner's imagination. This one contains a lot of bones, and some of them could easily be fossils, perhaps even those of dinosaurs.

(stones from the gizzards of many animals such as crocodiles and ostriches), believed to guard against poisons, displayed items such as iron nails from Noah's Ark, the jawbone of a Greek siren and demons imprisoned in blocks of glass.[1] Rudolf II became so obsessed with collecting oddities that he neglected affairs of state and eventually was forced to abdicate.

These collections were intended, above all, to inspire wonder, and they often gave impetus to speculation as well. Some collectors such as Scheuchzer specialized in fossils, which were often considered manifestations of a mysterious force called *vis plastica*, akin to spontaneous generation of plants and animals. Bringing large numbers of fossils together for comparison gradually enabled people to study them more systematically. But its origin in collecting, rather than in more unequivocally intellectual pursuits, placed palaeontology under a stigma, which it has arguably never entirely overcome. The preoccupation with dinosaurs runs through our society, but it is far stronger in popular media than in high culture. It is most visible in B-movies, science fiction and other genres aimed more at a mass audience.

The study of fossils in Britain and the rest of Europe during the early nineteenth century took place largely on the fringes of the scientific community. The major figures were amateurs with relatively little formal training for their vocation, who became obsessed with the

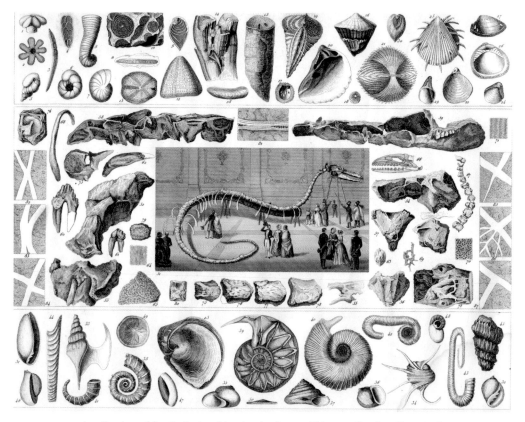

A collection of fossils depicted in a book of natural history of c. 1850. Even in the mid-19th century, fossils were still generally displayed in a rather unsystematic way, arranged mostly according to their value as curiosities rather than according to geological period.

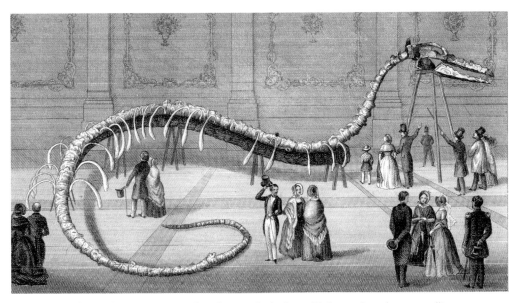

A detail of the previous graphic, showing finely dressed ladies and gentlemen strolling around what appears to be the reconstructed skeleton of a prehistoric lizard. Actually, it is a fraud, perpetrated by Dr Albert Koch in the 1840s by stringing together the vertebrae of several whales. The ambience of the scene is very ceremonious, almost to the point of being religious.

vestiges of early life that mining and construction projects had begun to unearth in ever-increasing numbers. They often looked enviously towards France, where the study was far more professionalized. Britain did not have any figure who was remotely as authoritative as Georges Cuvier, nor any centralized collection of materials pertaining to natural history that approached that of the Muséum National d'Histoire Naturelle in Paris. Nevertheless, the foundations of palaeontology were laid, perhaps for precisely those reasons, more in Britain than in France. The bold thinking which is required in the early stages of a discipline is often best accomplished outside of an institutional bureaucracy.

Much of the impetus came from the discoveries of Mary Anning (1799–1847), who is still probably the most legendary fossil hunter ever. She began collecting fossils in childhood along the Jurassic Coast

Picture of Mary Anning with her dog, Tray, 1842. In the background is the Golden
Cap outcrop in Dorset, where she found many of her fossils.

of Lyme Regis, Dorset, and, together with her father and brother, sold them to tourists. At the age of eleven, she discovered one of the first skeletons of an ichthyosaur. Her other finds include the first complete fossil plesiosaur and the first pterosaur discovered outside Germany.

Yet another major figure was Gideon Mantell, a country doctor who became so utterly obsessed with finding, collecting and interpreting fossils that they took up almost all the space in his house. His preoccupation with fossils eventually alienated his wife and children, but he first named and described the *Iguanodon* and the *Hylaeosaurus*, and partially identified the first known sauropod.

The most professionally distinguished of the early fossil hunters was William Buckland, who named and described the megalosaurus, the first dinosaur to be identified, and who with Anning also pioneered the study of fossilized faeces, known as coprolites. Buckland was also a quintessential English eccentric, who imitated what he thought were the sounds and motions of prehistoric animals in his lectures, and had his guests greeted by a pet bear in academic robes. In addition, he was a distinguished cleric, who eventually became Dean of Westminster. The lives of these pioneers are full of the misunderstandings, neglect and general chaos that often accompany forays into new intellectual territory. By the 1840s, palaeontology was well established, and institutional channels were clear. The emerging leader of the field was Richard Owen, who coined the name 'dinosaur', meaning 'terrible lizard', in 1842. He was dubbed the 'English Cuvier', and was known for not only his prodigious knowledge of anatomy but his penchant for indulging in personal feuds with his colleagues.

At the time, even the idea that prehistoric creatures could be given a place in current taxonomies was a novel one. The giants of the past still appeared so strange as to elude almost any scientific analysis. Debates had concentrated mostly on highly specific descriptions about matters such as their length and diet. Other scientists prior to Owen, including Gideon Mantell, had begun to intuitively group the creatures we know as 'dinosaurs' together, but Owen was the first to

Iguanodon, one of the three creatures originally identified by Richard Owen as 'dinosaurs', in an illustration from S. G. Goodrich, *Johnson's Natural History of the Animal Kingdom* (1874 edition), based closely on the Crystal Palace sculptures by Waterhouse Hawkins. The animals appear at least as mammalian as reptilian.

describe them collectively in a systematic way. Using the framework of Linnaeus, Owen proposed a class named *Dinosauria*, which initially contained only three genera: the megalosaurus, iguanodon and hylacosaurus. What distinguished these creatures from other prehistoric reptiles, as well as from modern ones, according to Owen, was that rather than having their legs splayed out to the sides, they were directly under the torso, much like those of mammals today. Owen also argued that they probably had four-chambered hearts and were warm-blooded.

Although he did not state it explicitly, Owen's taxonomy had a subtext, which was directed at early advocates of evolution such as Jean-Baptiste Lamarck. They had believed that animals are gradually transformed though the inheritance of acquired characteristics: a giraffe's neck, for example, became as long as it is because generations of these animals stretched upwards, trying to reach leaves at the tops of trees. They also believed there was an overarching trend in evolution towards creatures of ever-greater refinement and complexity. By showing that dinosaurs were not primitive lizards but, on the contrary, more advanced than contemporary reptiles, Owen endeavoured to demonstrate that biological progress, and therefore evolution, was an illusion.[2] By simply extending contemporary classifications to creatures of the remote past, Owen was saying that they were fundamentally similar to modern animals.

Mary Anning, Gideon Mantell and William Buckland had been driven to their discoveries by a relatively disinterested curiosity. Their work had been essentially a hobby, even if it at times became an obsessive one. Anning and Mantell had spent much of their lives close to the edge of poverty, while Buckland drew his income from a more lucrative

Hylaeosaurus, one of the three creatures originally identified by Richard Owen as 'dinosaurs'. Illustration from S. G. Goodrich, *Johnson's Natural History of the Animal Kingdom* (1874 edition), based closely on the sculptures by Waterhouse Hawkins. The animals appear at least as mammalian as reptilian.

source. Owen was the first professional palaeontologist in England, and he brought new status to the field. His predecessors had spent most of their time in the field searching for fossils. Owen spent most of his in an office, where fossils were brought to him for identification. This new standing of palaeontology was accompanied by an increase in academic intrigues, as different researchers tried to claim credit for the same discoveries. But nobody could have foreseen how, in the latter nineteenth century, it would also become an epicentre for struggles over glamour, money and power.

The Crystal Palace dinosaurs

Dinosaurs, perhaps alone among scientific subjects, have repeatedly been the subject of extravagant public displays, costing vast sums of money, employing renowned craftsmen and generating enormous publicity. The display that started this precedent was that of the Crystal Palace dinosaurs, which now appear like gargoyles from the ruined cathedral of human progress and culture. They had one important precedent, the Parco dei Mostri (Park of Monsters) near Bomarzo in Italy, commissioned by the wealthy mercenary Vicino Orsini at the height of the Renaissance in the mid-sixteenth century. This was arguably the world's first theme park,[3] and it featured enormous stone figures of mythological and invented beasts, intended to amaze and pleasantly frighten visitors. Included were dragons, sirens and a giant with an enormous mouth that visitors could enter. Whether or not this display directly helped to inspire the prehistoric beasts of the Crystal Palace, it provided much the same form of entertainment, and a comparison between the two illustrates how much the lore of dinosaurs owes to early myths and legends.

Today, the sculptures around the Crystal Palace tell us quite a bit about periods such as the Victorian era, though rather less about dinosaurs. The story of these models begins with the Great Exhibition of the Works of Industry of All Nations, an extravaganza planned largely by Prince Albert, which was designed to showcase technological marvels across the globe, as well as to demonstrate Britain's leadership in innovation. If there has ever been an event that marked the birth of modern, commercial culture, it is this spectacular display. Exhibits were housed in a huge building of steel and glass known as 'the Crystal Palace' in central London, which covered 7 hectares (18 acres) and incorporated six elm trees.[4] It anticipated the sleek, modernist architecture of the twentieth century, yet was created on the model of an Anglican cathedral, and parts of it were referred to using ecclesiastical terms such as the 'nave and transept'. Like the cathedrals and palaces of an earlier time, the Crystal Palace was intended to evoke wonder and amazement, by virtue of its splendour and grand scale. But, unlike the cathedrals, it was not built over centuries but in a mere seven months, in the timescale not of God but of commerce. It was perhaps indirectly intended to evoke the glory of God and of the monarch, but far more immediately that of manufacturing and trade.

A VISIT TO THE ANTEDILUVIAN REPTILES AT SYDENHAM—MASTER TOM STRONGLY OBJECTS TO HAVING HIS MIND IMPROVED.

Cartoon by John Leech showing a teacher dragging a terrified boy through an exhibit of the Crystal Palace dinosaurs, 1858. The dinosaurs were intended, like the 'house of horrors' at an amusement park, to scare people a little but not too much.

Dragon with a fish and lion, from the Parco dei Mostri near Bomarzo, Italy. Like the Crystal Palace dinosaurs, the dragon here combines fierceness with a touch of humour. It could almost be taken for a dinosaur.

The Crystal Palace was also promoted as a place of education, but, above all, it was an enormous shopping mall, with 14,000 vendors. It became a place of pilgrimage, and people of modest means would trek long distances simply to behold the edifice and perhaps buy a souvenir. Daily attendance averaged 42,831.[5] The Crystal Palace promoted an ideology of human progress, capitalist expansion and British supremacy, which, at the time, could seem to be almost the same thing. But what could that possibly have to do with dinosaurs? They seemed at first to symbolize everything that the Crystal Palace was intended to negate. They were the greatest of anachronisms, examples of savagery and remote times. Naturally, they could not be allowed within the hallowed precincts of the palace itself, but they were later added on the outskirts to dramatize how far humankind had come.

After the fair itself had ended, the Crystal Palace was moved to the South London suburb of Sydenham, where it reopened in 1854, together with a cohort of sculpted dinosaurs and other prehistoric creatures. The new incarnation of the Crystal Palace was not confined to science and technology, but endeavoured to represent all of human culture, in order to demonstrate how it culminated in the British Empire. Having largely subdued the globe, Britain was engaged in a conquest of the past, in which great kingdoms of yore were to pay it a sort of homage. The builders commissioned plaster casts of sculptures from across the world, and devoted exhibits to particular civilizations such as those of ancient Egypt, Assyria, Greece, Rome, India, China and so on. Each culture was granted its own rooms, with the dinosaurs and other prehistoric creatures placed outside the buildings in artificial islands yet organized according to the same principle, with groups that represented different periods in geographic history. While the sequence of both prehistory and civilization was very strictly linear, by representing divisions of time by locations in space, the display made them, in a way, contemporaneous. The palace itself, as a temple of civilization, was reserved for human beings, and the monsters were a bit like the statues of demons that guard the entrances to temples.

The models of dinosaurs and other extinct animals were constructed by a team led by Benjamin Waterhouse Hawkins, under the direction of Richard Owen. The dinosaurs were constructed around a grid of iron columns. One of them also required 600 bricks, 1,500 tiles, 38 casks of cement, 90 bushels of artificial stone, and other materials.[6] The length of a model iguanodon from the tip of the nose to the end of the tail was 10.59 metres (34.74 ft) and it had a circumference of 6.22 metres (20.40 ft).[7] The four dinosaurs were the centrepiece of the exhibition, but Waterhouse Hawkins also made models of many other prehistoric animals, from a pterodactyl and an ichthyosaur to a mammoth and an Irish elk. They were an enormous commercial success, with 40,000 people attending the opening ceremony of the theme park in 1854, and an average of 2 million visiting per year until the end of the nineteenth century.[8] It also made money, like several subsequent theme parks, by selling miniature models of the dinosaurs and other prehistoric creatures, as well as other souvenirs.

The dinosaurs, together with the other prehistoric creatures, were a project that approached such structures as the Brandenburg Gate, the Arc de Triomphe, the Lincoln Memorial, the Queen Victoria Monument and, for that matter, the Crystal Palace itself in ambition and scale. They were also built to last for the ages. In a mischievous mood, one might even see in the dinosaurs a parody of the rulers and generals for whom such massive monuments had usually been reserved. The same thing could be said of mounted dinosaur skeletons, which were just starting to become popular. But the dinosaurs were truly larger than life, at least than any life today, with the exception of whales. There had previously been nothing like the Crystal Palace dinosaurs, and they heralded a new status for both their subjects and natural history.

But the conventions of monumental sculpture also had the effect of making the dinosaurs overly formal, static and isolated from their surroundings, rather like bronze statues in a city park. The earliest depictions of dinosaurs, including the sculptures by Waterhouse Hawkins, show a world in which each creature seems to exist in isolation. There is no social or family life, in fact no coordination of any kind among the animals, even those of the same species. When the titans even take notice of one another, it is always for predation, which

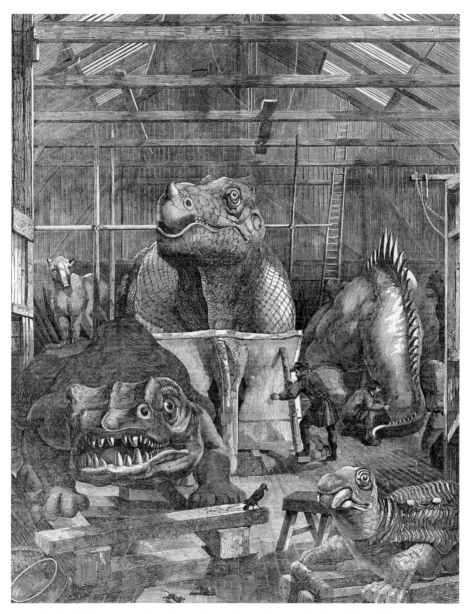

Benjamin Waterhouse Hawkins in his studio working on the Crystal Palace dinosaurs, *c.* 1852. With Victorian humour, the artist has emphasized the oddity of the creatures. He has also contrasted their fierceness with the apparent frailty of the man bending over in the centre-right of the picture, probably representing Hawkins.

Statues of labyrinthodonts at Crystal Palace Park, London. These dinosaurs
each seem disconnected from the rest, a bit like artworks in a museum.

is only subtly suggested and never actually portrayed. Viewers may
have perceived this isolation as primitive, but it was also suggestive of
modern individualism, even laissez-faire capitalism. Like virtually all
depictions of dinosaurs, it contained projections of human characteristics, which could inspire feelings either of fear, guilt or superiority.
The discovery of dinosaurs, like the Industrial Revolution, evoked
great hopes, but also stirred apocalyptic fears. The giant lizards
quickly attracted public attention, generating not only monographs
but cartoons, newspaper articles, additional theme parks and so on.
New discoveries were quickly absorbed into popular culture, which,
in turn, provided impetus, and direction, for further research.

Within a decade, new discoveries had rendered the Crystal Palace
dinosaurs scientifically anachronistic. They were not especially
beautiful, at least not in any conventional sense, and they certainly
did not convey any sense of high drama, but they have had a continued fascination for many people. What draws us to the sculptures

is probably much the same as what attracted the Victorians – their utter strangeness. Essentially, they are incongruous blends of slightly clichéd images depicting the exotic and mythological animals that so fascinated the Victorians. The iguanodon is a reptilian rhinoceros, while the hylaeosaurus has some resemblance to a Chinese or medieval European dragon. The megalosaurus blends a monitor lizard with some sort of carnivorous mammal. To me at least, the animal that it most resembles is the hyena, which also puzzled the Victorians, since it seemed to combine features of both canids and felines.

In 1868, Waterhouse Hawkins was invited by the Board of Commissioners in New York City to construct a new palaeontological museum in Central Park, devoted to the prehistoric animals of America. It was to be made of glass like the Crystal Palace, but with the models of prehistoric animals inside rather than on the grounds. Unlike the figures at the Crystal Palace Park, they were not separated

The Crystal Palace dinosaurs, from S. G. Goodrich, *The Travellers' Album and Hotel Guide* (1862). Set in a contemporary landscape, the extinct creatures seem displaced, and an element of alienation adds to their inherent strangeness.

from one another by water. The figures would be exhibited beneath an arch of iron supporting sheets of glass, supported by neoclassical columns on both sides. Hawkins accepted the offer, moved to America, and enthusiastically started work. A sketch he made for the planned palaeontological museum showed huge models of several dinosaurs. A group of tourists is passing in front, with only a small fence between them and the statues. On the other side of the exhibit is another fence with visitors round it, beneath an ornamented bridge. The figures are far more theatrical, predatory and anthropomorphic than those of the Crystal Palace Park.

As the iguanodons had been the centrepiece of the exhibition at the Crystal Palace Park, a hadrosaur, which was closely related to them, was intended to be the star of the new one. The drawing of it is six and a half to seven times the height of the tourists. The figure directly next to the hadrosaur in Hawkins's sketch is laelaps (later officially named *Dryptosaurus aquilunguis*), a therapod related to *Tyrannosaurus rex*. The two dinosaurs are exchanging glances, perhaps in an effort to intimidate one another. Not far away, Hawkins planned to have two other laelaps devouring another hadrosaur. As visitors walked through the museum they would pass through the aeons leading up to present time, encountering giant sloths, mammoths, Irish elk and other animals.[9]

Despite gaining wealthy and prestigious patrons, Waterhouse Hawkins never again even approached his popular success at the Crystal Palace Park, and one reason may have been that he did not understand the different symbolism of dinosaurs in America. His dinosaurs were like ghosts haunting a palace, but that was not how Americans thought of them. In Britain, the dinosaurs were an extension of tradition, adding to the age of the country by aeons. But America took pride in its wildness, even as it endeavoured to 'civilize' the land. The dinosaurs were, most especially, part of the 'Wild West', where nature still contested the territory with civilization. In short, Britain saw the dinosaurs as part of a glorious past. Waterhouse Hawkins may have failed to

Benjamin Waterhouse Hawkins's studio at Central Park. The picture shows a sly sort of humour. The dinosaurs and great mammals seem to be gazing at one another. The man standing in the background has much the same posture as the hadrosaurus on his right, and he is gazing straight out at the viewer.

realize that Americans saw them, on account of their vast dimensions, far more as a promise of a bountiful future.

Waterhouse Hawkins had been working on his models for two years when a corrupt administration controlled by 'Boss' William M. Tweed took control of New York. When Boss Tweed demanded that work on the museum be stopped, Waterhouse Hawkins complained and criticized him in a newspaper article. Tweed, supported by the mayor of New York, responded by sending thugs to break into Waterhouse Hawkins's studio, smash his models and throw the moulds into a nearby pond. One pretext suggested for the vandalism, and widely accepted at the time, was that the models were based on the theory of evolution, and therefore contradicted the Bible.[10] If the original Crystal Palace had been modelled after a church, the new one was a neoclassical temple, and the towering monsters could easily have suggested pagan idols. The vandalism may also have been partly due to hostility towards Waterhouse Hawkins as a prominent Englishman who had done much to promote Britain's prestige. The

An overview of the Crystal Palace dinosaurs after restoration in the late 20th century.
The space surrounding the dinosaurs is not nearly so elaborately landscaped as in
Victorian times, and the figures come across a bit like ghosts haunting a modern park.

Photograph showing the restored Crystal Palace iguanodons as they appear today.

Tammany Hall political machine was run largely by the Irish, and resentment between them and the English was strong. However, the major reason may have been simply that Tweed perceived the project as eccentric and, above all, unprofitable.[11] Waterhouse Hawkins went on to cast a skeleton of a hadrosaurus, which eventually became the state dinosaur of New Jersey, for Princeton University. He received similar commissions from other prestigious institutions in America, including several from the Smithsonian Institution, before finally returning to England in 1878.

The Crystal Palace was destroyed by a fire in 1936, and now only the dinosaurs, together with the other prehistoric animals, remain, newly restored and painted. We can take this as a reminder of the fragility of human accomplishments, as well as the ultimate resilience of the natural world.

'Bone Wars'

It is no coincidence that the first incontestable discoveries of dinosaurs had taken place in the same decade as the first railways, the 1820s, nor that both events took place in the country, the United Kingdom, that was then leading the world in industry. The early railway train was known as an 'iron horse'. Dinosaurs, trains and factories all roared, moved autonomously and had their own metabolism. The size and power of railways, huge cannons, warships and industrial machines also inspired awe. The British Empire and the increasingly globalized economy suggested, in their vastness of scale, the realm of enormous creatures. Dinosaurs were the past and the present, all of the things that inspired both dread and fascination in the Victorians – a mirror image of the age. The presence of huge machines and economies on a vast scale made dinosaurs easier to imagine, and they, in turn, made technology seem less unnatural.

The Crystal Palace Park firmly established the standing of dinosaurs as the totems of modernity, by virtue not only of their scale but

Contemporary stamps from Mongolia. Countries now see their dinosaurs as a part of national heritage and a source of status. Though a relatively small country, Mongolia takes special pride in being particularly rich in dinosaur bones.

of their association with commerce. By about the last quarter of the nineteenth century, dinosaurs had also become intimately associated with status and prestige. They became objects of competition between countries, industrialists, scientists and museums, and it was on rather childish terms that had no more than a peripheral relationship to science. Who had the biggest dinosaur? Who had discovered the most dinosaurs? Which nation was richest in dinosaurs? This juvenile competition also extended to the way people thought about dinosaurs themselves. Which one was the longest? The tallest? The fiercest? The fastest? Which dinosaur could win a contest of champions? Could triceratops beat tyrannosaurus? Could stegosaurus beat allosaurus?

The land of dinosaurs was the most exotic of realms, so, in the heyday of the British Empire, men could not help but dream of exploring and perhaps even conquering it. Nevertheless, since they were extinct, the dinosaurs also seemed to symbolize the lost grandeur of ancient kingdoms, as well as a warning to humankind. These conflicting analogies were not always comfortable to contemplate, and the Victorians often used dinosaurs to represent the reverse of how they wished to imagine themselves.

The decline of natural theology, which came as evolution gained wide acceptance in scientific communities, left the study of dinosaurs without much sense of purpose. Since they were so remote in the past, and the fossil record was fragmentary, dinosaurs initially played no more than a very minor part in debates about evolution. Darwin did not even mention dinosaurs in the initial edition of *On the Origin of Species*, and he only briefly referred to archaeopteryx in the fourth.[12] For a time, dinosaur studies became largely a matter of collecting and labelling exotica, as well as a source of many, usually implicit, metaphors for institutions and events.

But dinosaurs suggested the idea of life on a grand scale. Rulers and industrialists used them to dramatize what they thought of as the greatness of their agendas and accomplishments. This was especially true in the United States, which, by the late nineteenth century, was starting to rival Britain as an industrial power. From the early colonial days, Americans of European descent had been acutely conscious that they lacked cultural monuments, from castles to literary traditions, that could compare to those of the Old World, but they saw their wild, expansive landscapes, which seemed so full of promise, as compensation. The American Civil War was quickly followed by a massive westward expansion in which settlers laid railroad tracks and telegraph lines, slaughtered herds of buffalo and appropriated Native American lands. Like the British, Americans were devoted to what they saw as the ideals of progress and modernity, and the difference between the new world of 'civilization' and the old could hardly have seemed clearer to them. The land was littered with the whitening bones of buffalo and occasional cattle, which overlaid those of great mammals and dinosaurs.

When dinosaur bones began to be discovered in the latter 1860s and 1870s – in states like Montana, Colorado, South Dakota and Utah – it started a mad dash resembling the California Gold Rush of a couple of decades before. The pictures of the teams that excavated dinosaur bones certainly reflect the emerging fascination with the West. They are generally almost indistinguishable from those of cowboys, outlaws or lawmen – grizzled, unshaven men in well-worn, dusty clothes, with handlebar moustaches and cowboy hats, who are more likely to be holding a rifle than a shovel, let alone a pen. They look tough, rough and ready, and as though they would be far more at home in a saloon than a university lounge. This was certainly a long way from William Buckland, who hunted for dinosaur remains wearing academic robes.

Anyone who has ever worked in academia knows there are all sorts of tensions, jealousies and bitter rivalries simmering beneath

Charles R. Knight, *Leaping Laelaps*, 1897. Laelaps was one of the most popular dinosaurs, especially in America, around the start of the 20th century. These two are so fierce that their roughhousing threatens to exceed the bounds of play, and some think the painting is an allegory on the 'Bone Wars' of Cope and March.

The palaeontologist Othniel Charles Marsh, in the centre of the back row and surrounded by bodyguards and assistants, 1872. Marsh, who actually delegated the digging to others, alone carries a tool for excavating bones, while those surrounding him have weapons and seem to be spoiling for a fight.

the surface, and professors at times become obsessed with secrecy and intrigue. After all, it is often difficult or impossible to know, even with full openness and goodwill, how to apportion credit for an idea or discovery, and disputes about that often escalate into feuds. In the 'Bone Wars', however, all restraints fell away. In a frantic competition to get the most and biggest bones, the traditional dignity of scientific investigation was forgotten, to the horror of colleagues and the delight of a scandal-hungry public.

The two major figures were Edward Drinker Cope of the Academy of Natural Sciences in Philadelphia and Othniel Charles Marsh of the Peabody Museum at Yale University, who from the 1870s to almost the end of the nineteenth century launched well-funded expeditions to recover the biggest and best dinosaur bones available. The lurid story of their rivalry involved espionage, sabotage, bribery and even the destruction of fossils to prevent them from falling into rival hands.

Organic fossil remains of triceratops dinosaurs found in Wyoming. The dinosaur bones were found in unprecedented numbers in the northwestern United States around the end of the 19th century, generating a frenzy of competition for them among ambitious scientists and industrialists.

On at least one occasion, the two parties got into a brawl, and Marsh especially made sure to have strong men with him during excavations. Cope called a paper by Marsh 'the most remarkable collection of errors and ignorance ever displayed'. Marsh responded by saying, 'Professor Cope's mental and moral characteristics unfit him for any position of trust and responsibility.'[13] Both men exhausted their vast fortunes in the rivalry, but between them they discovered and named about 136 dinosaurs, including triceratops, allosaurus, diplodocus and stegosaurus.

Since Marsh discovered more dinosaurs, people have always considered him the winner of the Bone Wars, but this is a very crude criterion of distinction in science. Did the Bone Wars advance palaeontology? It is impossible to say for sure. The pressure of competition forced Cope and Marsh to work quickly, and they made many mistakes, some of which probably still remain to be corrected. They were also unable or unwilling to make very careful records of how and where their dinosaurs were found. Rather like prospectors for gold, they may have kept information secret and even disseminated falsehoods in order to keep rivals from important finds. Most of the dinosaurs would probably have been discovered eventually, and it is likely that slower, more careful work would have revealed more in the long run. Finally, and most significantly, the Bone Wars established precedents that promoted sensationalism, commercial success and personal aggrandizement over truth.

Carnegie's diplodocus

If you were to be a dinosaur, which would it be? For Andrew Carnegie, the answer was pretty simple – the biggest one! In November 1898, Carnegie, one of the richest men in the world, saw an article in the *New York Herald* entitled 'The Most Colossal Animal Ever on Earth Just Found Out West'. It showed a creature designated as a 'brontosaurus'. The article proclaimed that, 'When it stood up, its height was equal to eleven stories of a skyscraper.' The picture showed the giant sauropod standing upright on two legs peering through the top window of a high building. Other headings said that, 'When it ate, it filled a stomach large enough to hold three elephants' and 'When it was angry, its terrible roar could be heard for ten miles.'[14] Carnegie was impressed. He sent a note to William Holland, the director of his newly formed Carnegie Institute, saying 'My Lord – can't you buy this for Pittsburgh – try.'[15] The newspaper account turned out to be exaggerated, by some accounts a hoax, but Holland did manage to locate and purchase the skeleton of a giant dinosaur. Actually, it was necessary to combine bones of two individuals and then add a head made of plaster, but it could still reasonably be considered the biggest dinosaur ever discovered. The purchaser even managed to have it named after himself – *Diplodocus carnegii*. With the sort of hyperbole

Photograph of the mounted skeleton of *Diplodocus carnegii*, 1905. In the background is
Arthur Cogeshall, who once joked that it should be called the 'Star-spangled dinosaur',
since it was found on 4 July.

that was fairly common at the time, Holland called the mounting
and display of diplodocus 'the most colossal undertaking of its kind
in the history of the world'.[16]

About three years later, King Edward VII, son of Queen Victoria,
visited Carnegie at his summer resort, a castle at Skibo in Scotland.
The king saw a picture of the dinosaur and expressed the wish to
have one for the British Museum. Carnegie wrote to Holland, asking
about the possibility of obtaining one, and Holland wrote back that,
although finding another diplodocus would be extremely difficult, it
would be possible to make a duplicate using plaster casts.[17] Carnegie
granted the king's wish and sent a plaster diplodocus to the British
Museum, and then had additional casts made for museums in
Germany, France, Mexico, Austria and Argentina, though none for

any American museums. The diplodocus was, of course, a symbol of the excellence of American science. It established Carnegie himself as a man who, in his own right, could interact on fully equal terms with presidents and monarchs, almost as a second government in America.

Carnegie was a strong believer in the social Darwinism of Herbert Spencer, which carried over the biological idea of 'survival of the fittest' into the social realm, even though the tycoon tried to soften this philosophy by emphasizing the obligation of the rich to the public. He equated bigness, at least in dinosaurs, with superiority, much as he identified wealth with evolutionary success. The philosophy had been, from the start, little more than a jumble of vague associations, and Carnegie simply added one more. Anyone who was not dazzled by the glamour of money and power should have been able to see that gigantic size is not necessarily an evolutionary advantage. Furthermore, being the biggest did not necessarily make anything of greater scientific interest. The displays of prehistoric giants were actually not entirely different from a freak show at an amusement park.

The plaster cast of a diplodocus, gifted by Andrew Carnegie, in the Natural History Museum, London.

The era was one of grand ambitions, which transcended politics and ideology, and these were often expressed in sculptures, buildings and works of art on a gigantic scale. This was nowhere truer than in the Soviet Union, with its grandiose public ceremonies, monuments and public art. Its communism, however, was essentially a variant of the Victorian belief in continuous progress of humanity through history, and, accordingly, its artists – such as Vasily Vatagin and Konstantin Flyorov – tried to make prehistory appear as violent and savage as possible.[18] It became an illustration of 'predatory capitalism', the proverbial 'law of the jungle'. But communists have always admired the energy generated by capitalist methods of production, and that, too, comes out in the paintings.

Later, as the excitement that accompanied early industrialization gave way to two world wars and the Great Depression, dinosaurs in the West became identified with failure and extinction. Eventually, the Victorian era faded further into the past, becoming both an object of nostalgia and a spur for rebellion. It is often inaccurately idealized as a time of stability and robust values, and the countless books and dolls for children that feature dinosaurs usually appeal to that nostalgia.

Dinoland

Sinclair Oil sponsored Dinoland, probably the biggest dinosaur extravaganza since the Crystal Palace Park, at the 1939 and 1964 World's Fairs. Harry Sinclair had founded the company in 1916, and chose a heraldic brontosaurus (now usually called 'apatosaurus') as its logo in 1930, during the Great Depression. This was a time when big business was in ill repute, and dinomania was declining, but Sinclair used the symbol in a novel way. Instead of suggesting a glorious future for heavy industry, as it did for Carnegie, the dinosaur symbolized, in its association with the earth, a stable past. For Sinclair Oil, bigness no longer suggested dynamism or dominance, but stability. In a world where banks were failing and peace seemed ever more precarious,

Restored Sinclair Oil gas pump. The Sinclair Oil brontosaurus, proudly displayed on gas pumps, was among the most recognizable corporate logos of the mid-20th century, comparable to the golden arches of McDonald's.

Sinclair Oil was one thing you could rely on. By about the mid-twentieth century, constant proliferation of their images had given the dinosaurs a cosy familiarity. Everybody knew the 'important' ones like tyrannosaurus, brontosaurus and stegosaurus, almost the way we know celebrities. The current association of dinosaurs with children and families is due in large part to Sinclair Oil.

The brontosaurus logo was initially an allusion to a theory, now long discredited, that oil had been formed largely from the bodies of dinosaurs. In the latter part of the twentieth century, Sinclair Oil substituted a mystique borrowed from viniculture, suggesting that its oil had aged like a fine wine. In many advertisements, Sinclair Oil proclaimed that 'The mighty brontosaurus in Sinclair's trademark is a symbol of the age and quality of the crude oils from which Sinclair Petroleum Products are made – crudes which were mellowing in the ground when dinosaurs lived.'

But the giant of the industry was actually John D. Rockefeller's Standard Oil, which had long been taking over the other oil refining companies. Standard Oil had been declared a monopoly by the United States Supreme Court in 1911 and broken up, but Rockefeller retained control by holding shares in each of the successor companies. The Sinclair logo was probably deliberately intended to remind people of the diplodocus purchased by Carnegie, who had been one of the very few businessmen capable of competing with Rockefeller. Sinclair sponsored palaeontological expeditions, particularly those of Barnum Brown to find dinosaur bones in Asia for the American Museum of Natural History, thus suggesting an analogy between palaeontology and prospecting for oil. In return, Brown wrote pamphlets featuring dinosaurs for Sinclair Oil. In advertisements for Sinclair gasoline, a very anthropomorphic brontosaurus was often shown as a gas station attendant, standing on two feet with its tail in

A truck bringing the tripceratops to Sinclair Dinoland in 1964. Even in transit, the model dinosaurs often drew crowds.

...a hand in things to come

Reaching into a lost world
...for a plastic you use every day

Massive creatures once sloshed through endless swamps, feeding on huge ferns, luxuriant rushes and strange pulp-like trees. After ruling for 100 million years, the giant animals and plants vanished forever beneath the surface with violent upheavals in the earth's crust. Over a long period, they gradually turned into great deposits of oil and natural gas. And today, Union Carbide converts these vast resources into a modern miracle—the widely-used plastic called polyethylene.

Millions of feet of tough, transparent polyethylene film are used each year to protect the freshness of perishable foods. Scores of other useful things are made from polyethylene . . . unbreakable kitchenware, alive with color . . . bottles that dispense a fine spray with a gentle squeeze . . . electrical insulation for your television antenna, and even for trans-oceanic telephone cables.

Polyethylene is only one of many plastics and chemicals that Union Carbide creates from oil and natural gas. By constant research into the basic elements of nature, the people of Union Carbide bring new and better products into your everyday life.

Learn about the exciting work going on now in plastics, carbons, chemicals, gases, metals, and nuclear energy. Write for "Products and Processes" Booklet H, Union Carbide Corporation, 30 E. 42nd St., New York 17, N. Y. In Canada, Union Carbide Canada Limited, Toronto.

UNION CARBIDE

...a hand
in things to come

Advertisement for petrochemical products from Union Carbide in *National Geographic Magazine*, 1960. Advertisers of plastics, like those of gasoline, tried to counter the perception that their products were artificial by associating them with dinosaurs.

Newspaper advertisement for Sinclair Oil in the early 1960s
showing the brontosaurus standing on two legs and working as a genial
gas station attendant.

the air. Sinclair Oil sponsored dinosaur exhibits at many prestigious
events, including a 21-metre-long (70-ft) brontosaurus of fibreglass
at the 1933 'Century of Progress' World's Fair in Chicago. It marketed
dinosaur paraphernalia including booklets, toys and stamps.

For Dinoland at the 1964 World's Fair in New York, Sinclair Oil
refurbished the brontosaurus, and also featured eight additional new
or renovated fibreglass dinosaurs, including a 13.5-metre-long (45-ft)
Tyrannosaurus rex. All of the models were partially automated, and
contained motors which moved their necks and heads. Though the

Newspaper advertisement for Sinclair Dinoland at the New York World's Fair, 1964.
The posture and facial expressions of the dinosaurs appear slightly melancholy, as
though they felt a bit awkward in a modern environment.

largest dinosaurs such as brontosaurus, tyrannosaurus and stegosaurus
were still shown dragging their tails on the ground, and a few dinosaurs
had their legs splayed slightly to the sides, smaller dinosaurs such as
struthiomimus and ornitholestes were fully bipedal and had raised
tails. The guidebook specifically described ornitholestes as 'alert and
active'.[19] This probably reflected the advice of John Ostrom, one of

An overview of Sinclair Dinoland, designed as something between a fantasy for children and a museum exhibition. Visitors could observe the dinosaurs from many angles, in a way that neither evoked fear nor inspired stories.

the exhibition's scientific consultants, who would later go on to argue convincingly that birds were descended from dinosaurs. But the general effect of the display, as with the Crystal Palace Park, was to fix the dinosaurs in static, heraldic poses in the public imagination. This impression was then further disseminated by countless advertisements in newspapers and magazines, standardizing the public perception of dinosaurs far more effectively than any scientific publication possibly could.

This display was the culmination of the industrial era in the symbolism and marketing of dinosaurs, which had begun with the Crystal Palace Park, and was pervaded by nostalgia for a vanishing world of childhood. Dinoland was a place where time had stopped, and with it all worries about age, disease and politics. While the Crystal Palace Park had placed its model dinosaurs on artificial islands around the perimeter, the Sinclair dinosaurs were directly in the World's Fair itself, demonstrating how completely the prehistoric monsters

Tyrannosaurus rex from the booklet published by Sinclair Oil to accompany its exhibit
at the World's Fair of 1964. The text explained that the dinosaur was 'the largest
and most terrifying flesh eater that ever lived' and that it 'reigned supreme for many
millions of years'. After such an introduction, the image may seem to be an anticlimax,
since the tiny arms seem awkward and the large belly is precariously exposed.

Image of a triceratops from Sinclair Oil's booklet. 'This tough-looking fellow
resembles a rhinoceros,' the text tells us, adding that it had a 'beak like a parrot'.
The artist has also given the creature stripes, a bit like those of a tiger.

had been domesticated. At the same time, the ideology of progress, while it still informed the entire exhibition, was not proclaimed so confidently. The fair was as much a celebration of nostalgia as advancement, and dinosaurs, representing a bygone era, seemed to fit in without any ambivalence. Perhaps even the idea of progress had, by that time, taken on a nostalgic appeal. On the Sinclair website

Image of a stegosaurus from the booklet published by Sinclair Oil for the 1964 World's Fair. The text calls the creature 'one of the oddest-looking of all dinosaurs'. The creature's legs are splayed out to the sides in a way that, given its bulky torso, seems incongruous.

Image of *Ornitholestes* from the Sinclair Oil booklet. Unlike its larger relatives depicted in other images, this dinosaur appears very quick and agile.

today is an advertisement in which a grandpa lovingly tells a little boy about a visit to Dinoland.

Six million people came to Dinoland, and 500,000 of them purchased toy dinosaurs.[20] Afterwards, however, Sinclair Oil sold or gave away all the fibreglass dinosaurs, and never again attempted such an exhibit. The company may have realized that societal changes and scientific theories would mandate changing the dinosaurs in any further displays, which would have interfered with their nostalgic appeal. In post-industrial society, the public, used to interacting with digital devices, would no longer be satisfied with dinosaurs that only turned their faces.

The oil industry has retained a strong connection with dinosaur studies, even though it has produced no recent symbol as recognizable as Carnegie's diplodocus or the Sinclair brontosaurus. David H. Koch, an oil magnate, has made gifts of tens of millions of dollars for dinosaur exhibits to both the Smithsonian Institution and the American Museum of Natural History (AMNH). Despite the fact that these institutions try to promote awareness of climate change, while Koch has sponsored campaigns to deny it, the dinosaur wing at the

John Margolies, Harold's Auto Center, Sinclair gas station, Route 19, Florida, 1979. There has long been a strong association of motor vehicles with dinosaurs and petrol with their bodies.

AMNH is named after him. The Duncan family, which made a huge fortune in oil and natural gas, is the major sponsor of the vast new palaeontology wing of the Houston Museum of Natural Science.[21]

Hi-tech dinosaurs

As the post-Second World War economic expansion continued, the public was less interested in security and craved, instead, thrills and excitement, which movies, with their Technicolor and increasingly sophisticated special effects, could offer far more effectively than contemporary electronic models. The exhibits by Sinclair Oil may have started many people daydreaming about living alongside dinosaurs, but a series of B-movies enabled them to experience that vicariously. In 1966, Warner Brothers released *One Million Years B.C.*, set at a time in which dinosaurs had actually been long extinct and human beings had not yet appeared. A poster for the movie proclaimed, 'Travel back through time and space to the edge of man's beginnings . . . Discover a savage world whose only law was lust! Recreated as never before – with all the realism, savagery, and scenic splendors captured on the giant screen in breathtaking color.' On one side of the picture, cavemen threw spears and rocks down from a cliff at an attacking tyrannosaurus, while on the other a brontosaurus was lifting a caveman in its jaws. In the foreground stood starlet Raquel Welch, wearing contemporary make-up and a tiny fur bikini. The film consisted of spectacular fights between people and dinosaurs, as well as natural disasters such as landslides and suddenly erupting volcanoes, loosely tied together by the story of a romance between 'Loana the Fair One', played by Welch, and a man from a neighbouring tribe.

This was followed by a similar film, entitled *When Dinosaurs Ruled the Earth*, by the same studio in 1970, starring Victoria Vetri in place of Welch. This time the poster showed a tyrannosaurus lifting a scantily clothed blonde girl in its jaws. A brontosaurus was attacking a pterosaur as a priest raised his hands in adoration, in a probably unwitting parody of dinomania. In the centre stood Vetri in a bikini holding a spear above the words, 'Enter an age of unknown terrors, pagan worship, and virgin sacrifice.' It was a combination of horror movie, beach party movie, disaster movie and soap opera. Some of the special effects were relatively crude, such as using a blow-up of an iguana as a dinosaur, but the stop motion animation was state of the art, and earned the film an Academy Award nomination.

But, with the digital revolution, models and other means of representation eventually caught up with film. Today, there are scores of large dinosaur theme parks scattered throughout the world. Dinosaur World, for example, is a chain of them, with branches in Florida, Texas and Kentucky. Each location features about two hundred plastic models of dinosaurs, a few as long as 45 metres (150 ft), in addition to interactive models. In Japan, the company Creature Technologies has created an enormously popular travelling exhibition of robotic dinosaurs, which is intended eventually to have a permanent home in an amusement park. Visitors can line up to be lifted in the jaws of *Tyrannosaurus rex*. In addition, there are countless smaller dinosaur theme parks

Scene from Dinosaur Planet, a theme park in Bangkok, Thailand.

alongside highways and in towns. For computer geeks, Crytek has created a program called *Dinosaur Island*, where it is possible to visit the world of dinosaurs in virtual reality. It has also created a computer game called *Jungle Dino*, where you can interact with, and control, pre-historic creatures. Yet another game is *Island 359*, created by the company Polygon, where you are placed on an island of dinosaurs, and the task is to kill as many as possible.

A local newspaper gives this description of 'Dinomania', an exhib-ition of robotic dinosaurs at the Milton J. Rubenstein Museum of Science and Technology in Syracuse, New York:

> The lights and sounds can be heard before stepping into the museum entrance, giving the sensation of visiting a real-world Jurassic Park. On the right is a robotic skeleton of a duck-billed dinosaur, fully controllable by visiting paleontologists, giving parents the opportunity to assure younger children that this is 'not real'. An apatosaurus mother feeds her young and also greets visitors. On the far left is a tenontosaurus being eaten alive by four deinonychus . . . A maiasaura mother feeds her hatching eggs nearby, while two pachycephalosaurs or 'bone heads' butt heads in a game of dominance. A lone triceratops stands on the side, waiting for visitors to mount it for a fun photoshoot, while the beast itself – the *Tyrannosaurus rex* – towers above the scene, its shrieking roar at close range is enough to raise the hair on the arms and run shivers down the spine.[22]

This exhibition clearly has far more resemblance to a 'house of horrors' at an amusement park than to a traditional museum display. It leaves almost no room for the visitor's imagination, but reinforces speculative, and rather stereotyped, ideas about dinosaur appearance and behaviour. It most certainly does not prepare young people for the cautious, repetitive work that science requires.

In addition, the late twentieth century brought a huge proliferation of dinosaur accessories, a phenomenon that began with the Crystal Palace Park. Early figures of dinosaurs sold to children had a staid dignity, and the manufacturers wanted to present them as models rather than 'toys'. They were in rather generic poses, which were good for showing their basic form, yet appeared stiff and immobile. The museums, which projected considerable gravitas, felt rather inhibited about aggressive marketing, but their hesitations gradually fell away in the second half of the twentieth century. The bronze replicas were replaced by plastic action figures of many colours, which might easily be set up to fight medieval knights or astronauts. Stephen J. Gould, himself a great dinosaur enthusiast, has complained 'about the inundation of kiddie culture with dinosaurs in every cute, furry, and profitable venue that any marketing agent can devise', adding that 'a dinosaur on every T-shirt and milk carton does foreclose any sense of mystery or joy of discovery – and certain forms of marketing lead inevitably to trivialization.'[23]

Since that was written, the marketing of dinosaur paraphernalia has become far more prolific with the Jurassic Park movies. They are not just *about* a dinosaur theme park; they *are* a dinosaur theme park: an elaborate, hugely expensive public display of prehistoric animals, produced in the name of science, yet intensely marketed with commercial tie-ins to toys and many other accessories. These include Jurassic Park baseball hats, sweatshirts, bumper stickers, keyrings, mugs, neckties, cellphone cases, shower curtains, refrigerator magnets and so on. The list is virtually endless. The films are the current heir to the tradition of the Crystal Palace Park and Sinclair Dinoland. The first movie alone cost more to produce, and then brought in far more money, than has ever been spent on palaeontology.[24]

With all the new techniques of animation, virtual reality and robotics, the fantasies that we create around dinosaurs will soon almost completely overwhelm the reality as reconstructed by palaeontologists, if that has not already happened. The Godzilla franchise is now well over half a century old and still going strong. The Jurassic Park franchise might be similarly durable, and generate movies with ever more sophisticated special effects, incorporating occasional references to spectacular dinosaur finds as well as assorted fashions. It is, however, hard to see how this could be done while maintaining even the pretence of presenting serious science. The house of illusions built on the foundation of dinosaur studies is a place where even an apatosaurus could get lost.

Popular culture has always borrowed very eclectically from many sources, including high literature, science and folklore, without paying special respect to any one of them. In areas such as entertainment and advertising, dinosaurs will become, as they were initially, essentially one more variety of monster. *Dungeons and Dragons* is a digital, role-playing game now produced by Hasbro, in which participants construct their own stories within a fantasy world containing necromancers and amazing creatures. Alongside various dragons taken from sources such as *The Arabian Nights Entertainments* or purely invented, it has included occasional dinosaurs. Its latest version is the game *Neverwinter: Tomb of Annihilation* (2017), prominently featuring not only dinosaurs but dinosaur zombies. The official announcement trailer for the game begins with a roaring *Tyrannosaurus rex*. According to Bruno Latour, 'The adjective "modern" designates a new regime, an acceleration, a rupture, a revolution in time.'[25] This rift is what has separated dragons from dinosaurs. But if, as Latour has argued, modernity is an illusion, so is the difference between the two.

CHAPTER V

The Dinosaur Renaissance

The Lord Yahweh says this to these bones: 'I am now going to make
breath enter you, and you will live. I shall put sinews on you, I shall
make flesh grow on you, I shall cover you with skin and give you breath,
and you will live; and you will know that I am Yahweh.' I prophesied
as I had been ordered. While I was prophesying, there was a noise,
a clattering sound; it was the bones coming together. And as I looked,
they were covered with sinews; flesh was growing on them and skin
was covering them . . .

BOOK OF EZEKIEL (37:5–8, JERUSALEM BIBLE)

Americans still remember the two decades following the
Second World War with a combination of nostalgia and
revulsion. The United States had an intense, almost messi-
anic sense of its mission as the leader of the 'free world', and was
enjoying the longest and greatest economic expansion in its history.
In the new medium of television, westerns celebrated the triumph
of civilization over lawlessness, while situation comedies showed the
pleasures of affluence. Entertainments such as *The Flintstones*, an
animated situation comedy on television in which cavemen ride dinosaurs to work, made the suburban affluence of the 1950s seem to be
part of an eternal order.

A scene from the cartoon *The Flintstones*. Dinosaurs here take the place of machines,
in an idealized depiction of the affluent suburbs of the United States during the 1950s.
In many ways, these creatures anticipate the 'smart' devices of today.

But this optimism barely concealed an intense undercurrent of terror, frustration and rebellion. The country was engaged in the Cold War with the Soviet Union, which created an atmosphere of constant fear and tension. Intellectuals in America and Europe often found the post-Second World War decades to be stagnant, as well as culturally empty and stifling. The civil rights movement challenged not only segregation but, indirectly, American claims to moral superiority. The United States appeared moribund in many ways, yet perhaps poised for a dramatic transformation.

The growing restlessness and frustration were reflected in Thomas Kuhn's book *The Structure of Scientific Revolutions,* published in 1962, which had an enormous influence on nearly every aspect of intellectual life. Prior to that book, most people had assumed that the progress of science was strictly linear. Researchers thought that today knowledge was accumulated in increments, and bold ideas were usually dismissed a bit scornfully as 'speculative'. According to Kuhn, scientific investigation took place within what he called a 'paradigm'. This was a comprehensive analytical framework, which determined the nature and direction of research. Once a dominant paradigm was established, research could proceed according to a routine, through the gradual collection of facts. But every paradigm would entail 'anomalies', or phenomena that did not quite seem to fit within the established framework. When these became too bothersome to ignore, there might be a scientific revolution or 'paradigm shift', such as transition to the heliocentric cosmos, Newtonian physics, evolution, quantum mechanics or relativity. Since paradigms were fundamentally incommensurable, the change from one to another could not be decided simply by empirical evidence, but required a drastic change in perspective.[1]

The idea offered an opportunity to ambitious scientists who wished to be remembered as more than collectors of data. The most celebrated thinkers were those like Copernicus or Darwin, who had not simply increased knowledge but inaugurated a new paradigm. People often contrasted the revolutionary scientists of the past (at least as they were described in popular textbooks), who would boldly defy Church and state, with their thoroughly institutionalized counterparts in contemporary universities.

But the major scientific innovators from the Renaissance to the start of the modern world had not proclaimed their discoveries as revolutions in science. Robert Bakker, Niles Eldredge and Stephen Jay Gould, by contrast, very consciously set about to create a revolution, a paradigm shift, in scientific thinking. Palaeontology had appeared stagnant to many researchers, a sort of glorified 'stamp collecting', and many felt the time had come for a major change. For well over a century, most of the energy in the field had been devoted to finding, identifying and assembling old bones, and far less to theoretical questions. The close ties of scientists to corporations and government, with their potential for corruption, was something that people in other fields generally tried to conceal, but in palaeontology that was out in the open. The presentation of dinosaurs to the public seemed too slick and commercial to be entirely credible, as well as tied to a social order that was starting to seem static and repressive.

The superiority of dinosaurs

The Dinosaur Renaissance began in the 1960s when John Ostrom examined a fossilized claw of the deinonychus, a dinosaur that he had discovered in Montana. He theorized that deinonychus had walked upright and been very energetic, and, on that basis, Ostrom revived Thomas Henry Huxley's theory that birds were descended from dinosaurs. His former student Robert Bakker went further in his 1968 manifesto entitled 'The Superiority of Dinosaurs', arguing that dinosaurs in general had been warm-blooded.[2] Bakker later elaborated on his ideas in far more detail in his book *The Dinosaur Heresies* (1986). By writing a volume that used a very colloquial style and disregarded the usual academic protocols, Bakker went over the heads of his colleagues and appealed directly to the public.

Jan Sovak, *Deinonychus, c.* 2006. This predatory dinosaur attracted popular attention around the end of the 20th century for its reliance on speed and numbers rather than brute force to catch its prey. Notice the formidable sickle-shaped claws on its paws.

Dinosaurs had originated at about the same time as, or slightly later than, mammals in evolution. Bakker found it noteworthy that these giants had been able to 'out-compete' their mammalian rivals, as evidenced by the fact that they were far larger and more diverse. The only possible explanation, he believed, was that dinosaurs had been warm-blooded, which would have enabled them to maintain a higher level of activity. Meanwhile, he claimed, the earliest mammals had lagged behind dinosaurs, since they remained cold-blooded and, therefore, relatively sluggish.[3]

Campaigns by African Americans for equality had begun to inspire parallel causes among people of other ethnicities. Accordingly, Bakker made the case for dinosaurs by arguing that they were victims of prejudice. He thought that the warm-blooded nature of dinosaurs ought to be obvious, but many had failed to see it because they were 'mammalian chauvinists'. Bakker was endeavouring to raise the status

Heading to the chapter on reptiles from *Johnson's Natural History of the Animal Kingdom* by S. G. Goodrich (1874 edition). The large creatures in the lower right and left are probably somewhat fanciful dinosaurs. In general, reptiles, including dinosaurs, were associated with dark, moist, dangerous places, especially tropical jungles.

of dinosaurs, but he was, ironically, only able to do this by proclaiming that they were like mammals of today. A mostly unstated premise of the book was that evolutionary lineages go through a fixed progression from primitive to advanced. Mammals, specifically human beings, are now furthest along, but the dinosaurs were once ahead of them.

Bakker's claim that dinosaurs had been stereotyped as sluggish and lethargic, and therefore needed intellectual defending, was half-true at most. The view is mostly associated with Othniel Marsh, who in 1883 called the brontosaurus (or 'apatosaurus') 'a stupid, slow-moving reptile'.[4] Marsh was also responsible for the idea, which Bakker especially inveighed against, that dinosaurs lived in swamps and used water to buoy up their huge bulk. Because they had become extinct, dinosaurs were at times also associated with anachronism and failure. Their earlier use by industrialists such as Carnegie to symbolize big business was held against them after the Great Depression. But, while sometimes popular, Marsh's view of dinosaurs, contrary to what Bakker claimed, had never taken on the status of an 'orthodoxy'. There had always been plenty of alternative perspectives from distinguished scientists such as Thomas Henry Huxley and Edward Drinker Cope. Bakker would project his categories back in time, regarding those who agreed with him, like Owen and Huxley, as rebels and those who did not as 'establishment'. In fact, one could hardly be less 'establishment' than Gerhard Heilmann, who, in the early twentieth century, had convinced most palaeontologists that birds did not descend from dinosaurs. He was an artist with no formal background in science, who arrived at his thesis by anatomical observation, and then developed it, with hardly any encouragement from professionals, through research.[5]

To an extent, dinosaurs had been depicted as sluggish, simply because their representation was constrained by the practical difficulties of mounting their skeletons for display. When the American Museum of Natural History first mounted the bones of *Tyrannosaurus rex* in 1915, researchers knew full well that the king of dinosaurs had not stalked prey on bended legs, relying on its tail for support. It may have been mounted in that pose in part to increase its height, making the display more impressive, but that was mainly because the bones were too heavy to be supported in any other way.[6] This pose was then copied by many illustrators, making tyrannosaurus appear awkward.

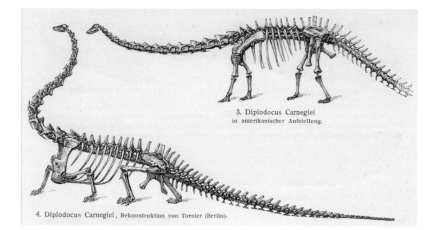

3. Diplodocus Carnegiei
in amerikanischer Aufstellung.

4. Diplodocus Carnegiei, Rekonstruktion von Tornier (Berlin).

Illustration to *Meyers Grosses Konversations-Lexikon* (Leipzig, 1902), showing two proposed reconstructions of diplodocus. The upper one has legs directly under its torso like those of a mammal, while the lower has them splayed out to the sides like those of a lizard. A consensus soon emerged that only the mammalian model could enable a dinosaur to support its weight.

Perhaps Bakker's biggest mistake was to assume that palaeontologists were solely responsible for the public image of dinosaurs, ignoring the huge role played by commerce and popular culture. To the extent that dinosaurs came across as sluggish and static, that was largely because of the way they had been stylized by the media. Their images, particularly that of the Sinclair Oil brontosaurus, had taken on a heraldic quality, which any hint of disorder or instability would have subverted. More broadly, the impression was due to the traumas of the twentieth century, most especially the First World War, the Great Depression, the Second World War and the Cold War. People did not always feel like contemplating bloody combats or apocalyptic extinctions. As long as sudden annihilation remained a constant, immediate prospect, many people may have found the extermination of the dinosaurs too frightening to envisage. Only when the Cold War drew to a close and the nuclear terror was partly, and perhaps only temporarily, lifted, were people prepared to take a look at the severe conditions under which their remote predecessors, the dinosaurs, had lived.

Dynamism and dominance

The rhetoric running through Bakker's writing was that of the counterculture of the 1960s and 1970s, and was becoming anachronistic when his book came out in 1986. His polemics played well in an era when the public was itself infatuated with novelty and youthful energy, though very often in a nostalgic sort of way. They helped to launch a major revival of the long-standing fascination with dinosaurs, with a new profusion of articles about them in glossy magazines, television specials and so on. Bakker nevertheless failed, at least in his immediate aim of changing scientific opinion, not because he was proved wrong, but because the terms of the debate had changed.

Animals that generate their own body heat are considered endothermic or 'warm-blooded', while those that rely on external sources of heat are ectothermic or 'cold-blooded'. Bakker assumed that ectothermy and endothermy were fully differentiated kinds of biological organization, and that dinosaurs must necessarily have been one or the other. This was in line with current opinion, which held that mammals and birds were endothermic, while reptiles, amphibians, fish, insects and all other animals were ectothermic. Researchers later realized that the two qualities exist on a continuum. Animals that fall near the middle such as echidnas, tuna, sloths and leatherback turtles are now called 'mesothermic'. Furthermore, the regulation of body temperature can vary at different stages of an animal's life, as well as by season. Hibernating animals such as bears and rodents become inactive and lower their body temperature in winter. In addition, many animals produce body heat in ways that are not easily characterized as either 'internal' or 'external'. Iguanas and many other lizards change colour in order to better absorb, retain or give off heat. Bees generate heat by shivering, while many fish produce chemicals that prevent them from freezing. Dinosaurs, particularly those that did not evolve into birds, did not necessarily all generate heat in the same way, and they may have had physiological mechanisms that are different from those of any contemporary animals.[7]

Bakker believed dinosaurs were dominant long ago, just as human beings are now, but 'dominance', like 'superiority', is a quality that cannot easily be defined in empirical terms. When Bakker and others speak of both dinosaurs and human beings as 'dominant', they are using completely different criteria of dominance for the two respective cases. Bakker and many others considered dinosaurs dominant in their era by the criteria of size and biological diversity, measures by which humankind would not score very highly at all. We are only moderately large, and we are represented by just a single species. Furthermore, we do not apply those criteria of dominance with any consistency to other species. There are about 375,000 species of beetles, vastly more than there are of mammals. Among terrestrial animals, the largest are elephants, followed by hippopotamuses and rhinos. Nevertheless, we never think of either beetles or elephants as 'dominant'.

The concept of dominance, in summary, is hopelessly vague and usually applied without even an attempt at consistency. It is misleading when Bakker says that the dinosaurs were able to out-compete the early mammals, as if both groups were endeavouring to become large and diverse. To human beings, dinosaurs certainly seem more impressive than early mammals, but both managed to survive for a long time. Perhaps the early mammals also did very well in their niche, limited though it may have been, much as rats are successful today.

Bakker constantly describes the reign of dinosaurs using metaphors of clans, dynasties and conquests,[8] blending the rhetoric of imperial expansion and capitalist competition. His dinosaurs and mammals come across a bit like the Soviet Union and the United States vying for global supremacy during the Cold War. In the decades after the collapse of communism, they suggest international corporations such as Microsoft and Apple. But Bakker's influence, as he may have intended from the start, was less on his fellow scientists than on a sort of dinosaur fandom. *The Dinosaur Heresies* had little direct impact on palaeontologists, but it inspired many palaeoartists, science fiction enthusiasts and collectors of dinosaur paraphernalia. By establishing parallels between dinosaurs and human beings, Bakker made it easier for artists, science fiction writers and many others to retell the story of those prehistoric giants as a grand epic, similar to that of humankind.

Why did Bakker care so passionately about whether a bunch of creatures that lived 65 million years ago or more were warm-blooded or not? Why, even more significantly, did he expect the public to care? He seemed to be intent on defending the honour of dinosaurs, almost as if they were still alive. Many people feel a sense of identification with dinosaurs, which can be nearly impossible to explain, especially in the language of science. I believe that Bakker mistook the spiritual affinity he felt between dinosaurs and human beings for the shared possession of an endothermic metabolism.

The punctuated equilibrium

An even more explicit, and more philosophically sophisticated, endeavour to create a paradigm shift in palaeontology appeared a few years after Bakker's initial article, in the 1972 essay 'Punctuated Equilibria: An Alternative to Phyletic Gradualism' by Niles Eldredge and Stephen J. Gould. Around the early twentieth century, an important school of evolutionary theory known as 'saltationism' held that evolution from one species to another occurs rapidly, but it had given way to Darwinian gradualism by the middle of the twentieth century. Eldredge and Gould revived it, claiming that most new species evolve relatively quickly, among groups of individuals that are reproductively isolated. They referred to this pattern of species remaining constant for long periods and then changing abruptly as the 'punctuated equilibrium', a pattern that parallels Kuhn's idea of a paradigm shift.

Their article did not introduce much new data, nor did it identify any previously unknown evolutionary mechanism. The argument that

Eldredge and Gould advanced was at least as much philosophical and historical as biological. That geographical isolation can abet the creation of new species has been known at least since Darwin and Wallace, but Eldredge and Gould claimed that this rapid sort of evolution was the rule rather than the exception. This, in their opinion, explained the apparent gaps in the fossil record that had been a serious problem for Darwin. Those who expected very gradual change would find the lack of transitional forms in the fossil record puzzling; those who were oriented to expect rapid change would not. The authors argued that their thesis would be apparent, if researchers had not been conditioned by tradition to regard evolution as slow. They needed to alter the terms of their studies since 'Science progresses more by the introduction of new world-views or pictures than by the steady accumulation of information.'[9] With their calls for abrupt change, the theories of Bakker, Eldredge and Gould launched indirect protests against the rigidity that many saw in both academia and American society as a whole.

The article continued to be debated for decades, but, as with Bakker's theory that dinosaurs are warm-blooded, the issues seemed to disintegrate during the debates. The theory could not be either proven or definitively refuted without first being made more precise, but that would have entailed sacrificing a lot of its meaning and almost all of its revolutionary power. Presenting their work as a paradigm shift had been a way to circumvent many petty objections in a sort of study where, as the authors rightly realized, the larger picture tended to get lost in a mass of detail. But, as the discussion proceeded, the authors had to add so many clarifications, qualifications and amendments to cover special cases that the theory lost its dramatic impact and, eventually, most of it relevance.[10] Genetic modifications, for example, are not necessarily immediately visible in a species, and do not necessarily show up in the fossil record. What seem like long periods of stability may, therefore, entail considerable change. Alterations that seem to appear abruptly may be a culmination of modifications that were not previously visible. Geographical isolation might be an effect, rather than a cause, of speciation. Like Bakker a bit before them, Eldredge and Gould had presented a model that was not so much wrong as too simple.

Gould and Eldredge knew that the gap in the fossil record that concerns people most is the one between hominids and humankind. While more than a century of intense searching has uncovered some transitional forms, these are not nearly enough to prevent human beings from seeming to stand dramatically apart from the community of animals. For creationists, that gap has been used to deny that people are a product of evolution, and, for almost everyone, it seems to confer on humankind a special status. But, according to the theory of a punctuated equilibrium, abrupt spurts of evolution were simply natural and, if anything, joined us with the natural world.

But it makes no sense to even talk about 'speciation' without a reasonably clear idea of what a 'species' is. The meaning of hierarchical categories such as 'genus' or 'species' is not very precise, even when applied to contemporary animals, and some biologists even think it is anachronistic. When Linnaeus first used them in the early eighteenth century, he thought they referred to natural divisions that were ordained by God. Today, 'species' usually refers to any group of animals that usually, though not necessarily always, only breed with one another; but distinguishing different species from one another remains a fairly subjective matter. Dogs show a huge variation in physiognomy, size and colour, yet, since all readily interbreed, they are put together in a single species: *Canis familiaris*. But, in any case, this distinction is impossible to verify with creatures that lived several million years ago. Were a palaeontologist from the remote future to excavate skeletons of our dogs, he would think that a Pekinese and an Irish wolfhound represented very different sorts of animal. Nobody is ever likely to know whether diplodocus and barosaurus could interbreed.

Eldredge eventually moved on to other things, but Gould continued to write prolifically about the idea of a punctuated equilibrium in a very popular series of essays for the magazine *Natural History*. Bakker had presented himself as an angry young man, while Gould came across as a genial elder statesman, but they both used a very personal tone, which earlier researchers would have seen as the antithesis of scientific objectivity. Gould believed, with Aristotle, that science is driven by a sense of wonder, and much of the appeal of his essays comes from this infectious enthusiasm. He would write with the same gusto of the elegance of an argument, the bones of a dinosaur, the arches of a Gothic cathedral or the swing of a baseball player. Advocates of natural theology in the eighteenth and nineteenth centuries, such as William Paley, explored nature and society with similar enthusiasm, but, unlike them, Gould did not see this sense of wonder as any intimation of a divine plan. He adopted the tone, but without the substance, of Victorian optimism.

For Gould at least, the punctuated equilibrium was a levelling device, a means to 'puncture' and deflate human pretensions, which interfere with our appreciation of the world. With respect to dinosaurs, this meant that, even though they might not be our contemporaries in time, there was no ontological barrier between us and them. To reduce the difference to a very simple formula, we might say that for Bakker, 'Dinosaurs are us.' Gould effectively reversed that to proclaim, 'We are dinosaurs.' Bakker saw the world of dinosaurs as essentially parallel to our own, and perhaps even extended a human sort of exceptionalism to them. To Gould, by contrast, both human beings and dinosaurs were simply episodes in the grand drama of all life.

The concept of a paradigm shift is still being intensely debated half a century after the publication of Kuhn's celebrated book. The most serious criticism of it, in my opinion, is that it distinguishes a bit too sharply between different paradigms and makes them appear incommensurable. As Martin Rudwick has put this, 'Even the changes of opinion that have often been presented as sudden, dramatic, and "revolutionary" . . . turn out, when studied closely by historians, to have been underlain by much more substantial continuities than those who counted themselves as victors wished their contemporaries to believe.'[11]

Science is actually very seldom, or never, conducted within a single dominant paradigm. The heliocentric cosmos, the geocentric one and Tycho Brahe's geo-heliocentric synthesis continued to be used alongside one another for centuries. Darwinians, Lamarckians and creationists all worked together on biological research for half a century at least, as they still do at times today. Around the middle of the twentieth century, many psychologists could move freely between the Freudian, Jungian, Adlerian, gestalt and behaviourist paradigms, depending on which seemed most useful in addressing a particular problem. Today, many physicists believe that quantum mechanics and relativity are ultimately incompatible, yet do not hesitate to use both. What people have traditionally taken for the 'foundation' may be, rather, one replaceable element in a matrix of interconnected observations, data, concepts, values, methods and other things that make up a scientific discipline. Rather than working from a single dominant paradigm, most scientists probably make use of at least three or four.

Bakker, Eldredge and Gould all saw their paradigms fragment and lose meaning as debates progressed, so they could not be properly accepted or rejected. These controversies in dinosaur studies were, however, followed by a dramatic proliferation of new discoveries in palaeontology. It may well be that Bakker, Eldredge and Gould helped to inspire this by shaking up a moribund establishment in their field. Other, less debatable, reasons include the availability of huge data-bases on fossils; the use of computer simulations; more powerful microscopes; and the new attention to dinosaur remains in places that had previously been neglected, such as China, Russia, India, Argentina and Australia. The basic pattern here extends far beyond the confines of palaeontology, since knowledge in virtually every area is now growing at an exponential rate.

Dinosaur studies today

Theorists are very hard-pressed to keep up with the constant influx of new information. Not only theories but even the vocabularies that are used to express them are in constant danger of obsolescence. Like all other academic fields, dinosaur studies is now divided by specialization, approach and region to a point where it is difficult to obtain an overview of current knowledge. It is even harder to formulate the sort of pithy summary that could serve as an 'orthodoxy'. 'Dinosaurs are . . .'. It is not easy to complete that sentence in any way that is simple, significant and interesting yet does not invite controversy.

Today, every year brings important new discoveries about dinosaurs. About 85 per cent of non-avian dinosaurs have been named just since 1990.[12] Since about the mid-1990s, scores of dinosaur remains, particularly in northeastern China, have been found with imprints of feathers. These quickly became a staple of popular depictions, which at times made dinosaurs appear almost like birds of paradise.

For about a century and a half, dinosaurs had been usually, though by no means always, portrayed as solitary. This did not reflect any particular theory, and there are several possible reasons for this. They were modelled in part on lizards, which are usually not very social animals. The depictions may also have reflected early ideas about man in the 'state of nature', before the covenant that created human society. Finally, they may have reflected the individualism of an era in which the lone cowboy riding into town was the archetype of manliness. But in 1979, palaeontologists discovered a nesting site of maiasaura, a hadrosaur (duck-billed dinosaur) in Montana. Several layers of nests were preserved, indicating that the dinosaurs formed a herd and nested in the same site over generations. This showed that dinosaurs were capable of complex forms of social organization, a theme that was quickly taken up in both scientific and popular culture.

A public image of dinosaurs was first established by the Crystal Palace Park in Victorian times, which emphasized their strangeness

as incongruous composites of many exotic creatures. It changed in
the early twentieth century, as conventions for representing dinosaurs
were established, first by murals such as those of Charles Knight
in museums of natural history and later by Sinclair Dinoland. The
emphasis was then on their vast scale. While the Crystal Palace Park
dinosaurs represented Britain and her empire, the new ones represented giant corporations, which constantly 'devoured' smaller ones
and occasionally battled with one another. The image of dinosaurs
changed again as the twenty-first century approached, this time
largely inspired by the Jurassic Park movies. As enormous factories
gave way to digital technologies, the archetypal dinosaurs seemed to
be no longer giants like *Tyrannosaurus rex* but smaller birdlike carnivores
such as deinonychus and velociraptor that hunted in packs. This was
not unprecedented, for one of the most popular dinosaurs around

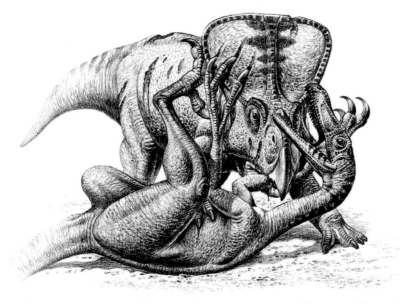

Raúl Martín, protoceratops fighting a velociraptor, 2003. One of the most celebrated
fossils ever, found in Mongolia in 1971, was formed as a velociraptor had grasped
a protoceratops with its talons, while the protoceratops grabbed a forearm of the
velociraptor in its jaws. Before either dinosaur could become victorious, a collapsing
dune buried them both. This image is a reconstruction of what transpired.

Edward Drinker Cope, 'Laelaps', *American Naturalist*, III (1869). Already in the latter 19th century, dinosaurs, including even fierce predators like laelaps, were at times depicted with affection. The creature on the far right is elasmosaurus, and the picture reflects a youthful error by Cope: he placed the skull on the end of the tail.

the start of the twentieth century had been laelaps, a relatively small therapod that resembled deinonychus.

These nimble therapods suggested the initially smaller, more agile and adaptable companies such as Microsoft and Apple, which were out-competing the giants such as AT&T or IBM. But today Apple and Microsoft are among the giants, and *Tyrannosaurus rex* still rules. As late as 2000, the last year for which figures are available, the Google Ngram Viewer showed that tyrannosaurus was still being mentioned over five times as often as deinonychus in books. The unique, elemental appeal of dinosaurs derives largely from their combination of size and antiquity, and it is unlikely that either research or publicity can change that. Even the movie *Jurassic Park* showed the king of dinosaurs making his entrance at key moments.

Almost every month I read of something like the discovery of a possible ancestor of the dinosaurs or an attempt to redraw the dinosaur family tree. But nobody ever speaks of these ideas as ushering in a paradigm shift, and they cause very little disruption in the scientific establishment, beyond the inconvenience of rewriting textbooks. Scientists have learned to better accommodate rapid change and to be more accepting of alternative views. They realize more clearly that scientific knowledge is only provisional, and subject to constant revision on every level, from empirical observation to the abstractions of theory. People in the decades immediately following the Second World War often felt stifled by what seemed to be an overly rigid social order, but today we are more frightened of chaos. Perhaps that is another reason why thinkers no longer emphasize the 'revolutionary' quality of their ideas, in dinosaur studies or any other field.

The debates in dinosaur studies in the latter twentieth century closely parallel those in literature, inspired largely by the philosopher Jacques Derrida, starting at about the same time or perhaps just a few years later. Like their colleagues in dinosaur studies, scholars of literature were worried that their area of study was amateurish and lacked

Painting by Jan Sovak, *c.* 2006, showing a maiasaura, whose name means 'good mother lizard'. Several maiasaura nests were found together, indicating that dinosaurs had a more complex social life than several earlier researchers had believed.

the status of a fully constituted academic discipline. It had no particular methodology and no professional vocabulary. What is more, it was largely focused on relatively simple factual matters such as explicating literary references. Also like the young palaeontologists, rebellious literary scholars tried to correct these limitations by asking bigger questions and using more highly refined abstractions. But, in both literature and palaeontology, the theoretical debates of the latter twentieth century now seem to be more of an interruption than the wave of the future.

The importance of theory has not increased in palaeontology, and it may be that its place has been partly taken by computers, which also order vast amounts of information. The focus on individual fossils has largely remained in palaeontology, though researchers can now easily compare their finds with several thousand others across the world. With computer simulations, it can become a little hard to tell just where research leaves off and entertainment begins. The heavy use of digital devices has increased the symbiosis between dinosaur studies and popular culture, as images of dinosaurs are used in video games, virtual reality and robotics. This continues to give the field of palaeontology glamour and to bring in funding, but it may still stigmatize it slightly as frivolous in professional circles.

Perhaps the most tangible result of the Dinosaur Renaissance has been in the area of palaeoart, specifically the visual depiction of dinosaurs. This was originally a branch of natural history illustration, but is becoming a more autonomous activity, enjoyed for its own sake rather than to enhance a book or exhibition. But, while major art museums have been increasingly open to subjects on the boundaries of art such as fashion in clothes, I know of none so far that has mounted an exhibition devoted to palaeoart.

Nevertheless, since the Dinosaur Renaissance, palaeoartists have felt increasingly free to openly speculate about what the habits and appearance of dinosaurs might have been. Carl Buell continues the tradition of Rudolph Zallinger, depicting dinosaurs with very careful

Carl Buell is arguably the most popular palaeoartist of the early 21st century, in part because his art is comparatively cheerful and optimistic. He does not emphasize portents of impeding extinction or bloody combats. Most of his scenes are set in bright, sunny landscapes, and even his scenes of predation seem playful.

Illustration by Carl Buell showing a *Parasaurolophus walkeri*. Many dinosaurs are famous for a single, dramatic feature, and here it is the large crest covering the head and protruding backwards.

attention to detail, but with an expanded palette of colours and a wider range of poses. John Gurche suggests stories in his pictures, particularly of predators facing off against their intended prey. Jan Sovak dramatizes dinosaurs through subtle but intense contrasts of light and shade, while Luis Rey depicts them in bright, and unabashedly fanciful, colour. Dougal Dixon even invents new dinosaurs. Few palaeoartists have deliberately used dinosaurs to comment on contemporary issues, but the late Ely Kish depicted them with great pathos to dramatize the dangers posed by climate change.[13] Dinosaurs are now often depicted with brightly coloured feathers and in highly active poses, even when this is not necessarily mandated by scientific research.[14] In addition, artists have to contend with the restrictions imposed as knowledge grows both more extensive and rapidly

Jan Sovak, painting of *Kentrosaurus, c.* 2006. Recent palaeoart focuses not just on the dinosaurs themselves but on the landscapes in which they lived. In the work of Sovak, the play of light and shadow is placed in the service of storytelling.

Luis Rey, tryannosaurus alongside a giant chicken, *c.* 2000. A vivid imagination has helped to make Rey one of the leading palaeoartists of the 21st century.

obsolescent. Furthermore, they now face competition from digital media, as well as the temptation to subordinate art to technology.[15]

What can we know?

It may seem paradoxical today that the rise of science was accompanied by that of religious fundamentalism. It is also a bit odd that it should have come in the West, where the traditional religious cosmologies were less scientific than those of Buddhism or Hinduism. The Asian religions had always incorporated a concept of deep time, as well as a fluid differentiation between animals and human beings. The reason why modern science developed in the Occident may be that Western cosmology of the early modern period, because of its very rigidity, provided a template against which it was possible to check observations.

The Creation narrative and the story of Noah and the Flood, in the Book of Genesis, when interpreted in a more rigid, fundamentalist way, gave people a framework in which to interpret observations of the natural world. The biblical account provided a seemingly unchanging constant, against which later developments might be measured. As confidence in literal interpretations of the Bible declined, other constants were needed to take their place. For early Darwinians, these were geographical processes, which theorists such as Hutton and Lyell thought of as eternal. As ever more constants, including the nature of space and time, have been placed in question, science has become increasingly abstract and arcane. But the necessity for scientists of justifying their work to the public set limits to this esoteric character, most especially in dinosaur studies, where visual images are so important. As the point of convergence between scientific and popular culture, dinosaur studies have always been pervaded by special tensions.

Our language, whether popular or scientific, was developed to describe the world as experienced by anatomically modern human beings. When it is extended to encompass realms of experience that are very remote from us, like that of dinosaurs, fundamental concepts such as 'species' and 'warm-bloodedness' start to collapse, and stand in ever-greater need of clarification. This is even more true of highly abstract and value-laden ones such as 'superiority'. Even our usual conceptions of time can no longer be taken for granted, since measures such as days and years no longer appear constant. Premodern cultures may have sensed this intuitively, and perhaps that is why they made almost no attempt to describe the conditions that existed more than about 10,000 years ago at the most. In the modern era, we have projected our categories back into the very distant past, and had spectacular success in describing it in extremely detailed and nuanced ways. But even our most sophisticated reconstructions of remote times involve unstated assumptions and unexplained concepts.

We can only describe and measure change through comparison with things that remain constant, which may be units of measurement such as days or feet or qualities such as fierceness. If we describe a dinosaur such as *Tyrannosaurus rex*, it will be in terms of innumerable implicit comparisons with creatures of the present day. If we call the creature 'huge', that is by contrast with terrestrial animals that are now alive. If we call it 'scary', that evokes images that are more varied and personal.

As we go ever further back in time, the apparent constants appear more questionable. Dinosaurs lived millions of years ago, but years are made up of days, so what if the earth did not always spin at a constant rate? In fact, scientists now believe it has slowed considerably over aeons. They now make their most precise measurements of time by the rate at which radioactive elements decay, something that would not even have been comprehensible to people a few centuries ago. To talk about geological time in such terms is still often too cumbersome and counter-intuitive, even for scientists. And how, in any case, can we be so sure that this decay happens at a constant pace? I must leave such esoteric questions to professional philosophers. My point for now is that, when it comes to imagining dinosaurs and their world, we constantly run into epistemological problems.

What this discussion shows, above all else, is how intimately the study of dinosaurs is linked with larger cultural trends. We still stylize the dinosaur world in many contradictory ways, all of which are a partial image of ourselves. It is doomed, since the large dinosaurs died off, yet also hopeful, for smaller ones evolved into birds. It is rigid, since most dinosaurs ultimately failed to adapt to global changes, yet it is also flexible, since they assumed a vast range of forms. It is wonderful, since it offers many parallels to human society, yet it is terrible, for precisely the same reason. In every case, dinosaurs are stand-ins for humankind, because they were at once enormously powerful, yet helpless in the face of cosmic forces far more powerful even than they.

The term 'Renaissance' refers primarily to a renewed interest in Graeco-Roman deities and other features of the classical world, particularly in Italy during the fourteenth and fifteenth centuries. Dinosaurs in the modern era have played a role that parallels that of pre-Christian divinities during medieval times, and dinomania was a way of paying homage to the fundamentally unknowable, elemental powers that humankind had tried to banish or domesticate. As I write this, hurricanes Harvey, Irma and Maria have just devastated parts of the United States on an unprecedented scale. They are in part a product of climate change, which has been caused largely by human activity, and remind me a bit of dinosaurs escaping from a theme park. Though they are exploitative and even tawdry in many respects, the Jurassic Park books and movies contain a serious message about the limits of human control. Once summoned, those powers, like the dinosaurs, cannot be contained within the walls that human beings erect. The franchise undercut that message through its rampant commercialization, but the theme may develop in ways that its creators could never have anticipated.

CHAPTER VI

The Totem of Modernity

'You're not allowed to call them dinosaurs any more,' said Yo-less.
'It's speciesist. You have to call them pre-petroleum persons.'
TERRY PRATCHETT, *Johnny and the Bomb*

W e cannot help but think of dinosaurs as, in some sense, contemporaneous. The intricate chronologies with which scientists order the succession of living things simply cannot be internalized. With respect to the human imagination, there is not very much difference between 65 million years ago (from the extinction of the dinosaurs till now), 180 million years ago (since dinosaurs first walked the earth), 200,000 years ago (since the emergence of *Homo sapiens*) or 4.5 billion years ago (since Earth was formed). All are far too vast periods of time to comprehend, and the years seem to blur together if we even try. Deep time easily becomes a sort of eternal present.

According to the historian of religion Mircea Eliade in *The Myth of the Eternal Return*, the irrevocable finality of the linear view of time, as proclaimed in Judaeo-Christian religion, evokes a terror that can only be assuaged by the promise of redemption at the end. This may be a mystical apotheosis, as in the biblical Book of Revelation, or it may take a secularized form, as it does in Marxism. The latter may

American postage stamp featuring the popular comic strip *Alley Oop*, originating in 1932, about a Neanderthal man who lives alongside dinosaurs.

take the form of a vague belief in 'progress'.[1] But, according to Eliade, the prospect of continual change without any ascertainable meaning, direction, goal or purpose is intolerable to most people. The history of dinosaurs seems to confirm this, as people constantly endeavour, in various ways, to deny the finality of their extinction, if often only in fantasy. Popular, and even scientific, literature is full of narratives in which dinosaurs survived in remote parts of the world or were recreated by human beings. There is also a strong tradition of time travel to the Age of Dinosaurs in fiction, including works by H. G. Wells, Ray Bradbury and many others.[2]

According to a Gallup poll taken in 1990, 41 per cent of Americans believe that human beings and dinosaurs lived at the same time.[3] Human beings and dinosaurs interact with one another in comic books such as *Alley Oop* and cartoons such as *The Flintstones*, as well as in movies like *Jurassic Park*. In 2008, the History Channel ran a series called *Jurassic Fight Club*, in which two computer-generated dinosaurs such as deinonychus and tenontosaurus would engage in combat, while human announcers would discuss their strategy and tactics, in the format of a boxing match. There is an entire genre of books known as 'dinosaur erotica', with titles like *Taken by T. rex* and *Ravished by Triceratops*. Many Christian fundamentalists believe that most dinosaurs died out about 6,000 years ago because Noah did not take them into his ark, but that he did save a few and that those may still be alive today. A huge model of the ark may be seen at the Creation Museum in Williamstown, Kentucky, complete with stalls that house model dinosaurs.

Already by 1856, when the official *Guide to the Crystal Palace and Park* was published, it was stated that pterosaurs were 'most probably the fabled dragons of old',[4] implying that they had been seen alive by human beings. Shortly after the opening of the park, the famed naturalist Philip Henry Gosse argued that many sea serpents reportedly spotted by mariners were actually plesiosauri.[5] Since the nineteenth century the Loch Ness Monster in Scotland has usually been depicted as a plesiosaur, as have similar legendary creatures reported at lakes throughout much of the world. There have been at least hundreds, probably thousands, of alleged sightings by mariners of the Great Sea Serpent, which continue to the present, and several also describe it

Sea serpent, from Hans Egede's *The New Survey of Old Greenland* (1734). The fins on this creature suggested to Philip Henry Gosse that it, together with other reported sea serpents, was a surviving plesiosaur.

as having the enormous eyes that are the most dramatic feature of an ichthyosaurus.[6] Arthur Conan Doyle once claimed to have seen a surviving example of that species.[7] The Mokele-mbembe, which is imagined as a giant apatosaurus, has been widely reported in Central Africa for over a century, and rumours of it have been enough to terrify entire villages.[8]

Even scientists can't entirely resist the idea of communing face to face with dinosaurs and have suggested ways to bring them back, if only half-seriously. Since the late twentieth century, there has been a controversial campaign to bring back extinct animals by cloning them using DNA. The most serious candidate is probably the passenger pigeon, which only became extinct in the early twentieth century. A more ambitious goal would be the woolly mammoth, which became extinct less than 10,000 years ago. But cloning a dinosaur stood out as the ultimate challenge, and that became the foundation for Michael Crichton's two hugely popular Jurassic Park novels, as well as the blockbuster films based on them.

Sea serpent, illustration to *The Romance of Natural History* by Philip Henry Gosse (1860). The harsh, desolate landscape and the luminous rays of light are common motifs in illustrations to the Book of Genesis, as well as in palaeoart.

Reconstruction of the Loch Ness Monster as a plesiosaur, outside the Loch Ness Centre, Scotland.

Since the novels, scientists have become more aware of the limitations of DNA. For one thing, it is unstable, and, even under favourable conditions, half of a strand of DNA will decay within 521 years. Fragments of it might still survive after a million years, but the non-avian dinosaurs became extinct 65 million years ago. Furthermore, DNA is not by itself sufficient to determine the course of an organism's development, but does this through interaction with its environment.

Palaeontologist Jack Horner has proposed an alternative way in which, theoretically at least, it might be possible to recreate dinosaurs, in his book *How to Build a Dinosaur: The New Science of Reverse Evolution* (2010). Birds are descendants of dinosaurs, so a chicken embryo might still contain the potential to develop into one. One might tweak the embryo by exposing it to a series of protein molecules, in order to

Gustave Doré, Friar John encountering a sea monster, 1873, illustration to Rabelais'
Gargantua and Pantagruel. Note that the creature has gigantic eyes that resemble those of
an ichthyosaurus.

make it develop into an ancestral form. But Horner admits that it
would be virtually impossible to know just what sequence would be
correct or even tell if a given outcome was the same as an ancestral
dinosaur. Furthermore, even in the almost impossible eventuality
that we managed to create a dinosaur in this way, it would still be just
an ancestor of the chicken.[9] It would not be one of the giants like

Illustration by Fernand Besnier to *Le Monde avant la création de l'homme* by Camille Flammarion (1886). The motif of a dinosaur standing on its hind legs and peering through the window of a tall building would be repeated in many popular publications in the decades to come.

diplodocus or tyrannosaurus, and those have always been, and still are, the ones that really appeal to our imaginations.

We are far less likely to think of the passenger pigeon or the dodo as belonging to the present than a dinosaur, because we place the recently extinct birds in a clearly defined historical context, with customs appropriate to their time, technologies and dress. We cannot reconstruct how the world of dinosaurs appeared with anything close to the same confidence and precision, so we think of them as outside of time. By pushing the age of dinosaurs so far back in the remote past, we have made them seem almost contemporary.

Modern culture

W.J.T. Mitchell has written, 'the dinosaur can best be understood as the totem animal of modern culture, a creature that unites modern science with mass culture, empirical knowledge with collective fantasy, rational methods with ritual practices.'[10] To summarize Mitchell's position briefly, we use dinosaurs to encode a wide range of ideas about society. He also points out that dinosaurs have an ancestral position with respect to humankind, since an Age of Reptiles preceded the Age of Mammals. Finally, the craze at times called 'dinomania' bestows on dinosaurs a magical aura, surrounding their excavation and display with all sorts of rituals and taboos.[11] According to Mitchell, the dinosaur 'epitomizes modern time sense – both the geological "deep time" of paleontology and the temporal cycles of innovation and obsolescence endemic to modern capitalism'.[12] Dinosaurs are often shown fighting, and they are always competing with one another for survival, much like modern businesses and empires. Their story is told in terms of successions of species, theories and geological eras, like those of the fads and fashions in capitalist societies.

More broadly, the modern era is characterized by the ever-growing commodification of time, which is divided increasingly into units which may be bought and sold. Wristwatches, initially not much more

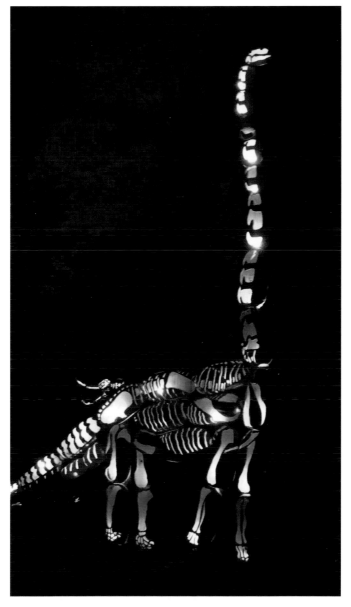

Apatosaurus made of lighted pumpkins, 2016. Dinosaurs figure prominently in the annual show entitled 'Blaze' at Van Cortlandt Manor in Croton-on-Hudson, New York, showing a dazzling display of figures from legend and history constructed primarily of jack-o'-lanterns.

A metal dinosaur sculpture in front of the Memorial Hall Museum in Deerfield, Massachusetts, serving as a mascot for an exhibition on geology and dinosaur footprints.

than a status symbol, gradually became a nearly universal accessory. Factories required workers to punch in and out with time clocks, and just about everybody had their lives regulated by increasingly elaborate schedules. An objectified idea of time was superimposed on our subjective, fluid experience of it.

At the least, Mitchell has identified a very intimate association between dinosaurs and modernity. That era is, most obviously, characterized by the rise of heavy industry, economies of scale, capitalism, state socialism and dramatic ruptures with tradition. Dinosaurs were discovered, or perhaps socially constructed, around the beginning of the nineteenth century, as the modern era began. This happened primarily in Britain, which was the unchallenged leader of the world in industry and commerce, though other industrial powers such as France, Belgium, the Netherlands and Germany also made substantial contributions. As America started to emerge as the world's foremost industrial power in the late nineteenth and early twentieth centuries, it also became the leader in collecting and displaying dinosaur bones. More recently, as China has challenged the United States for the status of the world's largest economy, the centre of dinosaur studies is shifting to it as well.

Our mythic ancestor

'Totemism' is one of those concepts that cannot be used with absolute precision, yet are too rich to be dismissed as incoherent. In the approximately one and a half centuries since it was first used by anthropologists, it has been repeatedly redefined, discarded, forgotten, neglected and revived. It refers to some sort of intimate bond between a species of animal or plant and a group of people. For theorists of the nineteenth and early twentieth centuries, a totem was generally the mythical ancestor of a people. Claude Lévi-Strauss challenged that idea. In *The Savage Mind* and other works, he explained totemism as a way of ordering human society on the model of the natural world. Totemic societies, in other words, read the natural world, with its differentiations into different animals and plants, as a sort of diagrammatic model used to describe relationships within human society.[13]

For the most part, Mitchell takes his inspiration from Lévi-Strauss, but one serious objection to that conception of totemism is that it assumes an abrupt differentiation between the realms of nature and humankind.[14] If the two were not very distinct, one could not serve as template for the other. But this division of the world, while characteristic of the modern West, is relatively foreign to most indigenous cultures. The partition seemed reasonable when Lévi-Strauss was writing, but research over the past several decades has revealed that human beings had an important role in forming what once seemed to be absolutely pristine environments. Amerindians of North America managed the landscapes around their settlements by starting fires on the plains, preventing trees from growing there. Parts of the Amazon were once filled with human settlements and cropland. Even the concept of 'wild nature' turns out to be a human construction, and animals that seem to embody it, such as deer, have actually lived in a close symbiosis with human beings for centuries or millennia.

But this does not apply to Mitchell's application of totemism to dinosaurs. We can rightly think of dinosaurs as Nature (with a capital 'N') at her most pristine, uncontaminated by human activity. Ironically, perhaps, Lévi-Strauss's conception of totemism may fit there better than anywhere else. Dinosaurs can never be our pets, and never help us with work. Nothing we can do will jeopardize or protect them. The study of dinosaurs will not help us to cure or prevent any disease, nor is it likely to have very immediate implications for contemporary ecology. Whatever practical implications the study of dinosaurs may have are remote and indirect, to a point where they are at least close to being philosophical. But precisely because dinosaurs do not impact human interests, they easily absorb human meanings. The old duality between nature and civilization, which ran though almost all Victorian thought, is now almost contiguous with that between the very remote past and the present. Today, all things have become 'human': back then, all things were 'dinosaur'. The Mesozoic era has become a template for understanding our own. When we gaze in that mirror, a dinosaur stares back at us.

But, in many respects, Mitchell is clearly not using the word 'totemism' in the same way as Lévi-Strauss or any anthropologist. He concedes that totems are usually familiar animals, while nobody has actually ever seen a dinosaur. He also adds that dinosaurs can function as totems, precisely because we, unlike most indigenous peoples, disavow their mystical function in the name of science,[15] consigning their numinous qualities to the unconscious. There are further differences that Mitchell does not mention. We generally think of tribes or nations, not historical eras, as having totems. Mitchell seems to be

From the celebration of Chinese New Year in Chinatown, New York, 2017. The Chinese dragon combines features of many animals such as the serpent, stag, carp, camel and hawk, and its image was inspired, at least in part, by dinosaur bones. The Chinese dragon features prominently in New Year celebrations, perhaps anticipating the use of dinosaurs as the 'totem of modernity'.

thinking of modern people as a sort of tribe, in the larger community of humankind throughout the ages.

I would have liked a bit more clarification about what Mitchell means by 'modernism', since, like 'totemism', that is a notoriously ambiguous concept. Does it refer to all people and ideas of the modern era or simply to those who adhere to a certain philosophy? Historians usually date the modern era from 1801 to 1950. Literary scholars are generally a bit more flexible about dates, and many would place the end of the modern era a bit later, perhaps in the 1960s or even the early 1970s. But, by any system of dating, the modern era ended about half a century ago at least. With respect to dinomania, the era probably reached a culmination in 1964 at Sinclair Dinoland, which expressed dinosaurs' grandeur in a static, nostalgic way. But if the modern era was a new Age of Dinosaurs, what will happen to dinomania now that it is over?

Mitchell expects our fascination with dinosaurs to decline, leaving them as one more subject of arcane, academic studies. He sees the high point of the age not as Dinoland but *Jurassic Park*, the book and the movie based on it, and asks whether it could 'be the last hurrah of the terrible lizards, a premonition that they could disappear a second time?'[16] In his opinion, the book and movie were a culmination of more than a century and a half of dinomania, after which its possibilities may be exhausted. He also believes that by artfully exploiting so many aspects of the cult of dinosaurs in *Jurassic Park*, Crichton and Spielberg have revealed the contradictions on which it was based from the beginning, such as that between pure science and commerce.

What is a 'dinosaur'? And can we rightly apply the term to the monsters of the Crystal Palace, Sinclair Dinoland or *Jurassic Park*? Can we apply it to toys or the figures in video games? When Richard Owen first coined the term in 1842, he was not thinking in terms of evolutionary descent, but only of animals that seemed to be similar in kind. Though based on the study of anatomic structures, the judgement was ultimately intuitive. In the late 1880s, Henry Seeley divided dinosaurs into ornithischians, like stegosaurus and triceratops, and saurischians, like apatosaurus and tyrannosaurus, on the basis of their hip structure, a division that, despite some challenges, remains generally accepted today. This inspired an extended debate over whether the two groups were distinguished by a common ancestor, a question that palaeontologists now mostly answer in the affirmative. Should it turn out that dinosaurs are not a monophyletic taxon (a single species together with its descendants), the term 'dinosaur', from the point of view of scientists, would be revealed as part of a 'folk taxonomy'. This would, however, make hardly any difference to the public.

Arcane debates about anatomy and evolutionary descent are not terribly important to most people. Dinomania has never been just about dinosaurs, at least not those of the palaeontologists. It embraces several creatures that, strictly speaking, are not classified as dinosaurs, such as plesiosaurs and pterosaurs. It may not extend, at least not fully, to many dinosaurs that are not especially large and that lack dramatic features. Dinomania is about the creatures we think of as 'dragons'. In the modern era, people attempted to break abruptly with their past, to create sharp divisions between the dinosaur of science and the dragon of myth. But the dinosaur, at least in popular lore, has never been entirely scientific, and the dragon never entirely mythical. Both are, and have always been, based on blends of observation, conjecture, tradition and fantasy. Dinosaur toys, movies like *Jurassic Park* and other popular entertainments blur or even erase the boundary between the two.

The future of dinomania

Unlike Mitchell, I do not believe the public fascination with dinosaurs will go away any time soon. Their size alone gives them an elemental appeal, and there is nothing comparable in the entire history of life. Furthermore, they resonate with mythic traditions that go back to the beginning of history and probably before. But, as the modern era recedes further into the past, dinomania will take very different forms.

This brings us to the even broader question of what will follow, or has already replaced, the modern era. The word 'postmodern' began to appear around the mid-1970s, and usually referred to an extreme eclecticism, in which people freely borrowed styles, motifs and rhetoric from many different eras and movements. At the end of the decade, Jean-François Lyotard published the original French edition of *The Postmodern Condition*, which presented a comprehensive theory of postmodernism and has proved to be one of the most influential books of the twentieth century. According to Lyotard, the basic change from the modern era to the present is that 'grand

John Margolies, dinosaur by a castle, Santa's Village, Route 2, New Hampshire, 1996.
A major characteristic of postmodernism is the eclectic blending of styles, motifs and
periods. Here we have dinosaurs before a medieval-style castle at the imagined home
of an American-style Father Christmas.

narratives' no longer serve to legitimate our quest for knowledge.[17] These grand narratives include not only the glorified histories of institutions such as communism, fascism and American democracy, but also, and more fundamentally, of modern science. The grandest of all grand narratives is surely that of life through time, recounted in many textbooks and museum exhibits, in which evolution culminates in humankind. It is also within this narrative that dinosaurs acquire modern significance, as an anticipation of, and even a sort of template for, the rise of man. In such narratives, dinosaurs appear rather like failed human creations, like the men of bronze in Hesiod's *Theogony* or the people of wood in Maya myth. This tale, which is unabashedly anthropocentric, no longer inspires confidence.

In *We Have Never Been Modern* (1991), Bruno Latour has argued that the modern era has been marked by a series of technological, scientific, political, commercial and cultural upheavals, in which people have attempted to obliterate, or at least render irrelevant, the past forever. But, he argues, such a break with the past is never possible, and the discarded patterns and institutions constantly return in the context of the new regime.[18] The reappearance of dragons as 'dinosaurs' is certainly a good example.

Destruction followed by nostalgia is the rhythm of modernity. The American Revolution abolished aristocratic titles, yet the country soon produced an elite of the very rich such as the Vanderbilt and Rockefeller families, who built elaborate palaces, collected art, cultivated patrician tastes and often even married into the European aristocracy. Perhaps dinosaurs became the totem of modernity precisely because they were extinct. They were, in other words, all the things that moderns endeavoured to eliminate, but then missed, such as kings, aristocracy, indigenous cultures, religion, country ways and, above all, the natural world.

The anthropologist Philippe Descola has suggested yet another way of understanding 'totemism'. He sees it as referring to an ontology, in which the fundamental unit is neither the species nor the individual but a collective, including landscapes and many living things. This sort of understanding is found above all among the Australian Aborigines, who have arguably the oldest continuously existing culture in the world. The collectives may be centred on geographic features such as particular rocks or springs, and may be represented by specific animals such as the opossum or mantis.[19]

At this historical moment, the anthropocentric perspective of modernism is under attack from many directions, especially the environmental movement. It is widely blamed for many horrors and catastrophes over the last few centuries – from the near-genocide of Native Americans to nuclear weapons – which are now so familiar that they hardly need to be listed. Most recently, many people credit modernity with at least contributing mightily to the sixth great extinction in the history of Earth, in which half or more of existing species are likely to perish. As alternatives to modernity, many people have proposed ecocentric and biocentric perspectives, but these are usually no more than very vaguely imagined.

I believe that Descola's conception of totemism may give us some hint about how our relations with other creatures, particularly dinosaurs, might be structured in the decades and centuries to come. Perhaps we may see ourselves more in terms of collectives, not simply of species that are currently alive, but also of those of the past or the imagination. And dinosaurs, which partake of both, would certainly be included. Anthropologist Marshall Sahlins summed it up by the formula, mostly with reference to indigenous cultures, 'Kinship is mutuality of being.'[20] Unlike the apes, dinosaurs may not be our close biological relatives, but they are, nevertheless, in this sense our 'kin'.

As I noted at the beginning of this book, the idea of an age in the remote past dominated by huge, reptilian beings is common in myth and folklore. Dragons in medieval lore of the West were often solitary survivors of a pagan era. But the best analogue to our modern cult of the dinosaur is probably the Dreamtime of the indigenous people of Australia. This is an era when powerful, largely reptilian creatures such as Rainbow Serpent and Gonna, the monitor lizard, created the features of the world that we know. Geographical features such as large rocks or streams take on a significance in Australian myth that is in some ways comparable to that of dinosaur fossils in palaeontology – placing it in the present, and adding sensual immediacy.

This creation, however, is not only in the distant past but is forever being repeated, as the world is perpetually renewed. Like dinosaurs in contemporary culture, figures such as Rainbow Serpent are part of an eternal present. The indigenous people of Australia have at times even identified the ancestral creatures of the Dreamtime with dinosaurs. In the Cape York district of Queensland, they speak of a cryptid known as the 'Burrunjor', which resembles an allosaurus. In parts of North and Central Australia, they tell of a herbivorous creature called 'Kulta', similar to an apatosaurus.[21]

Perhaps the concept of 'totemism' must be somewhat personalized to be used, but I would not consider it meaningless on that account. The same might be said of other words such as 'love' or 'fear'. Two people may never use them in quite the same way, yet the terms still can help us understand one another. Mitchell's idea of dinosaurs as 'totems of modernity' is at least very paradoxical. The word 'modern' still suggests newness, and we associate dinosaurs with the very remote past. He is not using the word 'totem' in quite the same sense as Lévi-Strauss had before him or as Descola would a couple of decades afterwards. Without committing ourselves to any one formulation, the word directs us to many perceived parallels between the world of dinosaurs and our own.

We think of both as 'dominant' in a given era, though the genetic and morphological variation among dinosaurs corresponds to the unprecedented cultural variation among human beings. Their many species may correspond to our nations, tribes, cultures or vocations. Their fierceness resembles our ruthlessness towards other forms of life. Their size and power corresponds to our intellect. The perceived parallels direct us to differences, which are similarly dramatic. The

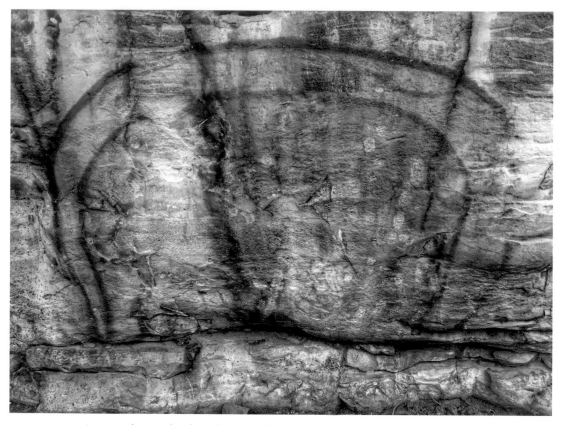

Ancient Aboriginal rock art depiction of the Rainbow Serpent, created *c.* 2,000 years
ago at Ubirr in Kakadu National Park, Northern Territory, Australia.

dinosaurs lasted about 175 million years, while anatomically modern
humans have only been around for a mere 200,000 years. The dinosaurs are extinct, while we now face multiple threats from sources
such as nuclear war and climate change. Maybe we should not speak
of them as 'ancestors', but I think we relate to the dinosaur as a sort
of 'big brother' of our kind.

CHAPTER VII

Extinction

I am become death, destroyer of worlds.

ROBERT J. OPPENHEIMER, on learning of the first successful test

of a nuclear bomb

'Big, fierce, and extinct.' That was the reply of child psychologist Shep White, when Stephen Jay Gould asked him why kids were so interested in dinosaurs.[1] This pithy formula does not apply exclusively to dinosaurs, and perhaps the same thing might be said of knights in armour or woolly mammoths. But it sums up the romance of dinosaurs very well. 'Big' and 'fierce' require little explanation beyond the desire for adventure. 'Extinct' is psychologically more complicated, and at first might seem to contradict the other two qualities. Grasping the reality of death is a gradual process for children, and one that people never entirely complete. Comprehending extinction is more complex, because it involves thinking in terms of eras following one another in a vast expanse of time.

Extinction is to a species essentially what death is to an individual. Nobody really comprehends death, but adults get used to the prospect, much of the time at least. Even today, the overwhelming number of children first learn about death through an animal. For 80 to 90 per cent of American children, the first confrontation with loss of a

loved one comes with the death of a pet.² Perhaps the dinosaurs, by virtue of being dead, seem to belong to the domain of departed pets, and that is certainly how they are usually presented by toy manufacturers.

That dinosaurs are extinct adds safety, as well as nostalgia, for both children and adults. We appreciate the passenger pigeon much better today than we did when it was common. Farmers used to regard the passenger pigeon as an agricultural pest. As species such as the Siberian tiger become rare and begin to approach extinction, they are not only more valued but can seem almost sacred. Our natural history museums are, in effect, mausoleums, with constant reminders of death, like stuffed animals, and extinction, like dinosaur skeletons.

The idea of extinction has never been entirely foreign. In Hesiod's *Theogony*, he speaks of three failed creations of humankind, which eventually became extinct. The philosopher Empedocles spoke of nearly endless combinations of heads, limbs and torsos of living creatures, only a very few of which managed to survive. Even the biblical story of Noah's Ark acknowledges extinction as a possibility, since it would otherwise have been unnecessary to preserve the animals in a boat. In the biblical Book of Revelation, the Beast is thrown into a burning lake (19:20), which might be a metaphor for extinction. A Jewish legend tells that there were once two leviathans, one male and one female. They were so huge and powerful that Yahweh feared that, should their number increase, they might destroy the world. He killed the female leviathan, but, so that the remaining one would not be lonely, God plays with it every day at dusk. When the end of the world approaches, that leviathan will be killed as well, and its meat will make a meal for the just.

But these were perhaps not extinctions in the modern sense, since they take place in mythic, rather than chronological, time. Linnaeus's

Gustave Doré, *The Destruction of Leviathan* (Isaiah 27:1), 1866. The leviathan is briefly mentioned a few times in the Bible, but it became the subject of many legends in Jewish and Christian traditions.

division of organisms into categories such as genus and species was, in effect, a theory of collective immortality, since it was based on the idea that forms of life had eternal essences which would prevent them from perishing or at least, if the conditions were right, enable them to reappear. Up to at least much of the nineteenth century, people widely assumed that, while individuals might come and go, these types would last forever. Thomas Jefferson, one of the first people in America to collect fossils, wrote in 'Notes on the State of Virginia' (1787), 'Such is the economy of nature, that no instance can be produced of her having permitted any one race of her animals to become extinct.'[3]

Bones of mastodons and mammoths had been dug up in the American colonies since the early eighteenth century, and Jefferson fully expected that an animal known then as the 'incognitum' or the 'Ohio animal' would be found eventually, disproving the Comte de Buffon's theory that the climate of the New World caused animals to degenerate in size. In 1803, when, as president, Jefferson sent Meriwether Lewis and William Clark to explore the Western states, it was partly in hope of finding the creature. But, at about the same time, in Paris, Georges Cuvier studied fossil remains of mammoths and mastodons, distinguished between them and concluded that they did not bear very close resemblance to any living elephants and must be extinct.

The theory of extinction

Cuvier was a scientist with an empirical orientation, who was renowned for his understanding of comparative anatomy and had little interest in theoretical speculations. In 1803, he was named permanent secretary of the Department of Physical Sciences of the French Academy. In that capacity, he had easy access to constant discoveries of bones from animals such as mastodons, giant sloths, pterodactyls and mosasaurs. In his *Essay on the Theory of the Earth*, he

Baron Georges Cuvier, who looks directly out at the viewer with a slightly melancholy expression. The fossil he holds serves as a sort of *memento mori*, perhaps even a reminder that all species may be subject to eventual extinction.

announced his hypothesis that animals eventually become extinct, which came to be known as 'catastrophism'. Earth had been populated in stages by animals that were no longer alive, exterminated in a succession of calamities such as earthquakes, of which the flood recorded in the Book of Noah was only the most recent. After each of these catastrophes, life had been created anew, except possibly for the last one, in which animals had been saved by Noah.

The violence of this vision, as well as the idea that life could be divided into many stages, was doubtless influenced, at least unconsciously, by the turbulence of Cuvier's times. As his career was becoming established, the *ancien régime* in his native France was overthrown. It was followed by a succession of revolutionary governments, the dictatorship of Napoleon and the restoration of the Bourbon monarchs. Cuvier had stayed aloof from politics and somehow managed to prosper under every faction. The sequence of governments imposed by revolutions, coups and conquests suggested analogous phases in the history of living things. In Cuvier's words, 'When a traveler crosses fertile plains . . . and where the land is never disturbed except by ravages of war or by the oppression of powerful men, he is not tempted to believe that nature has also had its civil wars, and that the surface of the globe has been upset by successive revolutions and various catastrophes.'[4] The successive episodes of violence and revolution, however, left Cuvier with a longing for stability. He was a devout Protestant who attended church regularly and considered early theories of evolution to be a danger to both reason and social cohesion.

If, as Cuvier believed, all life had followed a pattern of successive extinctions brought on by catastrophes, how might the subsequent creation of new life be explained? The inability to clarify this may be why the perspective of Cuvier eventually lost out to Darwinian evolution. Nevertheless, it made Cuvier's ideas attractive to many who wished to combine traditional religion with natural history, since it left plenty of room for divine intervention and guidance over the aeons. Rev. J. G. Wood, by far the most popular writer on natural history in the nineteenth century, wrote, in reference to the Mesozoic period:

> The huge saurians shake the ground with their heavy tread, wallow in the slimy ooze, or glide sinuously over the waters, while winged reptiles flap their course through the miasmatic vapors that hang dank and heavy over the marshy world. As with them, so with us – an inevitable progression towards higher stages of existence, the effete and undeveloped beings passing away to make room for new, loftier creations.[5]

Wood saw nature largely as a repository of religious and moral instruction, so the world prior to humankind held almost no further interest for him. All previous creatures had existed simply to prepare the world for men and women.

But it is not a coincidence that dinosaurs were discovered within a short time after Cuvier proclaimed his theory of extinction. Even though people were very slow to realize its implications, extinction may well have caused at least as much anthropological anxiety as evolution. The latter told where species come from, but extinction told where they were going in the end. Like that of evolution, the theory of extinction was at first very seldom applied to humankind. Darwin diplomatically refrained from mentioning human evolution in *On the Origin of Species*, only to take it up nearly two decades later in *The Descent of Man*. In a similar way, Cuvier himself never attempted to extend the idea of extinction to humankind. A sense of human exceptionalism was by then so ingrained that it was hard to imagine the species dying out. Only occasionally did people make this leap, usually not fully explicitly, in tones between anguish and nervous laughter.

Professor Ichthyosaurus

In Britain, Cuvier's major opponents were the 'uniformitarians' such as James Hutton and, later, Charles Lyell, who argued that the gradual work of natural forces over extended periods of time was sufficient to explain all the patterns and irregularities in the surface of the earth, without recourse to periods of upheaval and devastation. Just as Cuvier was influenced by the turmoil of recent history in his native France, they were influenced by the relative stability of their own government in Britain, which had for over a century seen steady economic and military expansion, with only comparatively minor interruptions. The debate between catastrophists and uniformitarians continues to this day, even though it is now mostly a matter of emphasis. From the start, both parties had much in common. They composed narratives extending over previously unimaginable periods of time, in which humankind was present only at the very end. They exulted in the grandeur of that vision, yet sought relief from its terrifying aspect by postulating a constant natural order. Together, the catastrophists and uniformitarians had prepared people for the gradual 'discovery' of dinosaurs in the first half of the nineteenth century.

The major opponents of Cuvier in his native France were the advocates of evolution, then known as 'transformationalism', Jean-Baptiste Lamarck and later Geoffrey Saint-Hilaire, who maintained that organisms, rather than going extinct, evolved into something else. The catastrophism of Cuvier was less threatening than it might have been, since it was easily compatible with the idea that living things have eternal essences that are not subject to change. Early theories of evolution at least saw biological lineages as potentially immortal. But when Darwin incorporated the idea of extinction in his theory of evolution, both became more emotionally threatening. They presented living things, including men and women, as fragile, perpetually contingent and perhaps even ultimately doomed.

Shep White's evocation of dinosaurs as 'big, fierce, and extinct' could be rephrased as: 'very much alive and completely dead'. From their discovery on, dinosaurs have always been closely associated with extinction, in a way that other vanished creatures from trilobites to mammoths have not. Dinosaurs have often been used metaphorically to describe anything that appeared doomed, such as the horse-drawn carriage after the advent of the automobile. But, by repeatedly mentioning their extinction, people implicitly emphasized how much dinosaurs' presence was longed for. The literature of dinosaurs is constantly pervaded by dreams of finding them alive in a remote part of the world, going back in time to their age or resurrecting them.

The discovery of deep time came at a historical moment when, in some ways, it appeared especially disconcerting. The late eighteenth and nineteenth centuries were an era of grand ambitions, when 'greatness' seemed almost synonymous with 'immortality'. Commanders like Nelson and Napoleon sought immortality through their deeds in battle. Poets like Shelley, Hugo and Tennyson strove to achieve it in their writings. Huge monuments of bronze, granite and concrete were constantly erected in honour of battles or famous people. But could such memorials mean anything at all in the perspective of deep time? If even mountains could not last for eternity, how could structures like the Arc de Triomphe in Paris or the Victoria Memorial in London? If even the human race would not last indefinitely, how could the British Empire?

The question of human fate was even more distressing than that of human origins. If other creatures, even those with the commanding presence of dinosaurs, had been destined for extinction, why should humankind be an exception? The possibility of human extinction added a special intensity to debates about evolution. If species had eternal essences, they might endure forever or at least re-emerge from oblivion. If species had appeared very gradually, and were in part products of chance, this was far less likely, and extinction had a nearly absolute finality. The dinosaurs became a template for considering a possible fate for humankind that was almost too terrifying to contemplate. They had been, like us, mighty in their day, yet left nothing behind but fragmentary bones.

In 1830 the palaeontologist Henry De la Beche produced a satiric lithograph entitled 'Awful Changes. Man found only in a fossil state – the reappearance of Ichthyosauri'. It shows an ichthyosaurus at a desk, dressed in an approximation of academic robes, wearing glasses and holding a pointer. He is lecturing to his pupils, an array of many prehistoric creatures including pterosaurs and primeval crocodiles, and possible dinosaurs. Beneath the desk is a stone, and lower still a small cavern, out of which peeks a human skull with a macabre grin, pointing its eye sockets directly at the viewer. Under the picture is the following caption:

A Lecture – 'You will at once perceive,' continued Professor Ichthyosaurus, 'that the skull before us belonged to some of the lower order of animals; the teeth are very insignificant, the power of the jaws trifling, and altogether it seems wonderful how the creature could have procured food.'

The mockery is immediately directed at a statement in Lyell's *Principles of Geology* that at some time in the remote future prehistoric creatures such as the ichthyosaur, the iguanodon and the pterodactyl might reappear.[6] Lyell saw the flow of time as essentially directionless, which put him at odds with the Victorian ideology of progress.

For all its farcical elements, the picture reflects a lot of covert anxiety. If you had asked a Victorian gentleman about it, he might

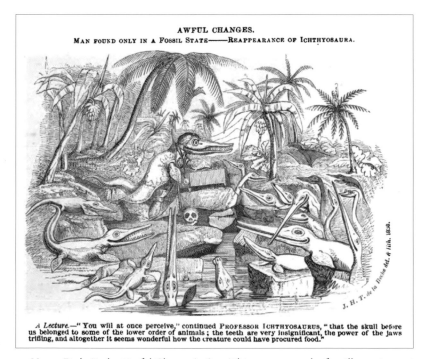

Henry De la Beche, 'Awful Changes', 1830. This was among the first illustrations that endeavoured to represent deep time, and, using humour to mask a good deal of anxiety, it showed one of the earliest references to the possibility of human extinction.

INDEAL IMPRESSION OF A FUTURE CREATION DISCOVERED BY PROFESSORS ICHTHYOSAURUS, MEGALOSAURUS, & ℮

'Ideal Impression of a Future Creation, Discovered by Professors Ichthyosaurus, Megalosaurus, &c.', humorous greeting card published by Thomas de la Rue in mid-19th-century Britain. The picture updates and responds to De la Beche's lithograph 'Awful Changes'. It reflects the responses of visitors to the dinosaur statues in Crystal Palace Park, who felt they had entered an alien world where they could never really belong.

have said something like, 'Of course, it is preposterous to compare a person to an ichthyosaur. And, to recognize the absurdity of the idea that people might become extinct, one need only consider recent human accomplishments – steamboats, factories, railroads . . .'. The extinction of man might have seemed almost as impossible to conceive as deep time had a couple of centuries before, but there was an incipient awareness of that possibility.

Human exceptionalism

The idea of human exceptionalism was so central to Victorian culture that any denial of it, even as an intellectual exercise, seemed absurd. One of the very few Victorians with the prescience and boldness to, at least briefly, confront the prospect of human extinction directly was the poet Alfred, Lord Tennyson, in his poem 'In Memoriam', which he published in 1850. What moved him to contemplate this radical idea was depression following the sudden death of his closest friend, Arthur Henry Hallam, from a cerebral haemorrhage at the age of 22. The poem, consisting of 103 strophes plus an epilogue, is a dialectic between grief and comfort. The poet considers many possible consolations, in nature, science, religion, and various forms of possible immortality, only to find them insufficient. Finally, he closes with a profession of faith in God, which seems hesitant but perhaps stronger for having survived many challenges.

Driven by grief, Tennyson went further than his contemporaries, to consider the death not only of a beloved friend but of all

F. John, *Protorosaurus speneri*, c. 1900. Even dinosaurs sometimes seemed a bit too modern for John. This is a picture of a reptile that pre-dates even them and survived the Permian extinction, which drove approximately 95 per cent of all species to extinction. John characteristically painted dinosaurs and other ancient animals in barren, rocky landscapes under fiery skies, at times with volcanoes in the background. Already around the beginning of the 20th century he saw their extinction as a warning for humankind.

Blatt No. 21. Eine der ältesten Urechsen ist Protorosaurus Speneri aus dem Kupferschiefer. Unser Bild stellt sie dar im Augenblick, wo sie einen Stachelhai (Menaspis armata) gefangen hat, ein Tier, das derselben Erdperiode (Dyas) angehört und mit gebogenen Stacheln gepanzerte Wangen besitzt.

F. John, the reverse side of the previous illustration, which was on a card advertising for a German chocolate company. For an advertisement, both seem uncharacteristically sombre. Here, a man contemplates a bone of an extinct creature as a *memento mori*, thinking perhaps of his own death or even the eventual extinction of humankind.

humankind. Death, at the time, was often referred to as 'the great leveller', since it did not observe distinctions of class or rank. The same might have been said of extinction, which would not necessarily be influenced by human pretensions to superiority. But, Tennyson asked, if the finest people are not free from death, why should men and women in general be exempted from annihilation?

In this connection, Tennyson makes one of the earliest poetic references to dinosaurs, or at least prehistoric giants, comparing them to human beings, in strophe 56:

'So careful of the type?' but no
From scarped cliff and quarried stone
She [Nature] cries, 'A thousand types are gone;
I care for nothing, all shall go.

'Thou makes thine appeal to me.
I bring to life, I bring to death;
The spirit does but mean the breath:
I know no more'. And he, shall he,

Man, her last work, who seemed so fair,
Such splendid purpose in his eyes,
Who roll'd the psalm to wintry skies
Who built him fanes of fruitless prayer,

Who trusted God was love indeed
And love Creation's final law –
Tho' Nature, red in tooth and claw
With ravine, shrieked against his creed –

Who loved, who suffered countless ills,
Who battled for the True, the Just,
Be blown about the desert dust,
Or seal'd within the iron hills?

No more? A monster then, a dream,
A discord. Dragons of the prime,
That tare [sic] each other in their slime,
Were mellow music match'd with him.[7]

Human beings might, then, eventually be no more than those bones
encased in the limestone of a mountainside. The term 'dinosaur'
had not yet been coined, and 'dragons' referred not only to them but
also ichthyosaurs, plesiosaurs and other giants of the remote past.
The image here is essentially that of artists like John Martin, of giant
lizards eternally tearing one another to pieces in a primeval swamp.

But, for all the despair and doubt, the poem never loses its decorum. The steady metre and rhyme seem to affirm the superiority of

civilization, even as the words place it in question. The poet had raised questions that neither he nor his contemporaries were emotionally very well prepared to deal with. Rather than pursue them, he would later go on to write about a nostalgic past of Arthurian knights and ladies.

Resurrection

In 1853, as the Crystal Palace dinosaurs neared completion, Waterhouse Hawkins decided to celebrate by hosting a New Year's Eve dinner party inside his sculpture of an iguanodon. Richard Owen, as the guest of honour, sat in the head of the dinosaur. The meal consisted of seven elaborate courses, after which the guests were treated to a vast and liberal assortment of wines. As the party continued well into the night, the guests joined in a song beginning:

> A thousand ages underground,
> His skeleton has lain,
> But now his body's big and round
> And there's life in him again!
>
> *Chorus*:
> The jolly old beast
> Is not deceased
> There's life in him again.
>
> His bones like Adam's, wrapped in clay,
> His ribs of iron stout;
> Where is the brute alive today
> That dares to turn him out? [Chorus]
>
> Beneath his hide, he's got inside
> The souls of living men;

Who dare our Saurian now deride
With Life in him again? [Chorus]

This idea was echoed in further verses, and Waterhouse Hawkins later recalled that 'the roaring chorus [was] taken by the company in a manner so fierce and enthusiastic as almost to lead to the belief that a herd of iguanodons were bellowing.'[8] The revellers were, in other words, bringing the dinosaurs back to life, in effect disproving the finality of extinction. And perhaps, if even an iguanodon might be spared, human beings had a pretty good chance as well. Such exuberance in a group of slightly stuffy scientists and officials is quite a testimony to the intensity of Victorian dinomania.

Banquet in the Crystal Palace iguanodon, New Year's Eve, 1853. The eye of the iguanodon seems to be gazing out directly at the viewer, as though the creature were indeed alive. From the *Illustrated London News*, January 1854.

This event shows that the fantasy of Jurassic Park was present almost from the beginning of palaeontology. I feel a bit hesitant here, and I may risk over-intellectualizing a bit of good-natured, drunken fun. But the song seems to have had plenty of passion behind it, and I cannot help but wonder in what way the revellers thought the iguanodon was still alive. They are equating the size and power of the iguanodon with the human ability to construct vast structures, which becomes the manifestation of a life force. The partygoers are also identifying themselves collectively with the monster and, by recognizing it, conferring new life.

At least for the rest of the nineteenth century, to even mention dinosaurs in literature was to invoke the themes of extinction and geologic time, as well as to question human exceptionalism, which explains why they were not mentioned often. Another example of one of the earliest references to dinosaurs in literature is the opening lines of Charles Dickens's novel *Bleak House*, first published serially in 1852–3:

> LONDON. Michaelmas Term lately over, and the Lord Chancellor sitting in Lincoln's Inn Hall. Implacable November weather. As much mud in the streets as if the waters had but newly retired from the face of the earth, and it would not be wonderful to meet a megalosaurus, forty feet long or so, waddling like an elephantine lizard up Holborn Hill. Smoke lowering down from chimney-pots, making a soft black drizzle, with flakes of soot in it as big as full-grown snow-flakes – gone into mourning, one might imagine, for the death of the sun. Dogs, undistinguishable in mire. Horses, scarcely better; splashed to their very blinkers.[9]

The reference to waters newly receded suggests a catacalysm, a great flood that catastrophists believed had destroyed some of the most primeval forms of life and opened the way for dinosaurs such as megalosaurus. The reference is soon followed by one to 'the death of the sun', a reminder that human time on earth, and even that of the sun, is limited. This passage is followed by several references to London fog, which obscures the images of dogs, horses and human beings. This is the proverbial 'mist of time', the deep time in which all beings are in a sense contemporaneous, and a megalosaurus ascends a hill in London. The image of a dinosaur or similar creature striding up a city street would later be taken up not in literature but in countless movies from *Godzilla* (1954) onwards.

After the promising yet fragmentary beginnings by eminent Victorians, the theme of dinosaurs just about disappears from high culture, including literature and painting, as mysteriously as the dinosaurs themselves did from the earth. The topic is taken up in fiction by authors who are closer to the popular end of the spectrum such as Jules Verne, Arthur Conan Doyle and Edgar Rice Burroughs in the late nineteenth and early twentieth centuries. Later, dinosaurs become even more popular in innumerable films such as *Godzilla*, *King Kong*, *Fantasia* and, finally, *Jurassic Park*, as well as public programmes and displays. Dinosaurs appeal, as previously noted, especially to kids, and, if my library searches are an indication, probably over 90 per cent of books written about dinosaurs are for children.

But I have been able to find no significant references to dinosaurs in works of high literature by major authors such as W. B. Yeats, T. S. Eliot, James Joyce, Virginia Woolf and many others. One possible explanation is that, linked closely with the theme of extinction, dinosaurs seemed particularly threatening to those who aspired to a sort of poetic immortality. For writers primarily concerned with making an immediate impact and perhaps achieving commercial success, this was less of a problem. For those more focused on an eternal human condition, and less easily content with thrills, the prospect of extinction was more difficult to contemplate. The uncompromising earnestness of high literature could make the themes of dinosaurs and extinction particularly difficult to address.

F. John, two primeval lizards, *c.* 1900. The orange sky is profoundly threatening and expresses apocalyptic expectations in the decades leading up to the First World War. One lizard takes refuge beneath a rock, while the other stays out to absorb the heat, a bit like people who confront an impending crisis respectively by withdrawal and active participation. Which of the two will survive?

Another explanation is that the late nineteenth to at least the mid-twentieth centuries were dominated by modernism in high culture, which emphasized both continuity with tradition and perpetual renewal. Ezra Pound's exhortation, 'Make it new!', was a slogan of the movement. Dinosaurs had been severed from tradition at the time of their discovery, when early palaeontologists refrained from classing them as dragons, and yet they were associated with the very distant past.

In the latter nineteenth and early twentieth centuries, the invention of photography was challenging traditional ways of representing reality, in the visual arts and, to an extent, even in literature. People questioned whether there was any point in realistic painting, when a photograph might convey the same information more thoroughly and with a lot less effort. But the challenge did not apply to palaeoart, since there was no way that anybody could take a photo of a dinosaur. As a result, palaeoart retained many conventions that went back at least to the Renaissance but were being energetically challenged by modernists. Though palaeoart was at times influenced by some movements such as Impressionism, there were no Futurist or Cubist paintings of dinosaurs. Palaeoart even continued to feature such old-fashioned media as the fresco, developed in the Renaissance, and its most celebrated works were arguably murals such as the ones by Charles R. Knight in Chicago's Field Museum and by Rudolph Zallinger in the Peabody Museum at Yale University. This adherence to traditional forms carried over into fiction.

As Joe Zammit-Lucia recently observed, 'the most general and characteristic feature of modern artistic production' is 'the tendency to dehumanize art'.[10] Movements of the early twentieth century such as Futurism and Cubism reflected an awe of industrial machines, and tried to reduce the human figure to its component forms. Later developments such as performance art may have rehumanized art in some respects, but their emphasis has been on society rather than the individual. Ironically perhaps, palaeoart, particularly the depiction of dinosaurs, by remaining aloof from modernism, may have preserved some elements of the humanistic inheritance that were abandoned in other genres. It consistently places emphasis on the individual – that is, on particular dinosaurs.

The neglect of dinosaurs in high literature effectively consigned them to the purveyors of commercial products, making them even less attractive to literati, creating a sort of vicious circle. In the words of Mitchell, 'One could hardly find a better exemplar of what Clement Greenberg called "kitsch" than the dinosaur's linking of commercial vulgarity with juvenile wonder and the imitation of past styles.'[11] This disregard exempted the depiction of dinosaurs in modern culture from the sort of relentless probing, exegesis and criticism that is

The palaeoart of Rudolph Zallinger is notable for its rich yet subdued colours and its meticulous attention to detail. Part of a mural painted for the Peabody Museum, Yale University.

The Hall of Dinosaurs at the Peabody Museum, with a mural by Rudolph Zallinger painted in 1947.

applied to important literary and pictorial innovations. The taboo against dinosaurs was not lifted until the latter twentieth century, as high culture and mass culture gradually began to merge.[12]

Godzilla

Human extinction had seemed little more than a theoretical possibility, though it had been written about by a few novelists such as Jean-Baptiste Cousin de Grainville and Mary Shelley early in the nineteenth century. The gradually increasing death toll of successive wars, which eventually exceeded all precedents, made the possibility seem a bit less unthinkable. Finally, in the Cold War, as the United States and the Soviet Union stockpiled vast reserves of nuclear weapons, the imminent prospect of human extinction became part of daily life.

In March 1954, a few months after the United States had first tested the hydrogen bomb at Bikini Atoll, a Japanese fishing boat named the *Lucky Dragon 5* drifted near the site. The fishers saw a bright light in the distance, and then an ashy powder covered them. At least one of them eventually died from radiation, and other people were exposed to it through fish sold at the market. The incident further stimulated still fresh memories of the atomic bombs dropped on Japanese cities. It also helped inspire the film *Godzilla*, released late in the same year by Toho Studios, in which a dinosaurian monster is used to represent the unpredictable forces released by nuclear bombs and war.

Though never identified specifically as a dinosaur, Godzilla has the plates of a stegosaurus and the general morphology of a tyrannosaurus, as well as forearms with grasping hands that resemble those of an iguanodon. It returns dinosaurs, however, to their folkloric roots in dragons. Like the Japanese dragon, it normally dwells far beneath the surface of the sea and has four claws. Japanese and other Asian dragons generate fire through the motion of their limbs; Godzilla, like a Western dragon, breathes fire from its mouth, not in the form of flame but as a radioactive beam.

The monster is awakened from the depths by nuclear testing, and ravages Tokyo. When a train collides with Godzilla, the vehicle is destroyed. The Japanese military try to kill the monster with bombs and with a huge electrified fence, but to no avail. Scientists are reluctant to participate in killing Godzilla, since they would prefer to study the beast. Finally, however, they agree to use the ultimate weapon, known as the 'oxygen destroyer'. The scientist Serizawa finds the monster under the sea and unleashes the weapon, then cuts off his own supply of air, thus dying with his victim and taking the secret of its destruction to his grave. The film ends with a warning that further nuclear tests could summon another Godzilla. The movie was a huge popular success, and has been followed by many sequels. Over the years, Godzilla became increasingly sympathetic. In some films, particularly *Godzilla versus Hedorah* (the Smog Monster), released in 1971, it became a protector of nature against the abuses by humankind.

With the threat of nuclear war between the United States and the Soviet Union, the theme of possible human extinction went from being an almost unmentionable topic lurking in the background to an obsession. People throughout the United States were told that a nuclear war might break out at any moment, and a siren would give them only about ten minutes warning before the bombs exploded. Children practised air raid drills in schools across America, where they would stand with their heads to the wall or crouch under their desks in hope that this might enable them to survive a nuclear blast. People with money would build air raid shelters, which they tried to make impregnable not only against the explosion but also starving neighbours.

As the Cold War started to wind down, that fear became less immediate, though it did not disappear. But the taboo against thinking of human extinction had been irrevocably broken, and people openly contemplated all sorts of ways in which this might occur. A few of these were fully immediate and real, while others, in various degrees, were speculative and even fanciful. Along with nuclear war,

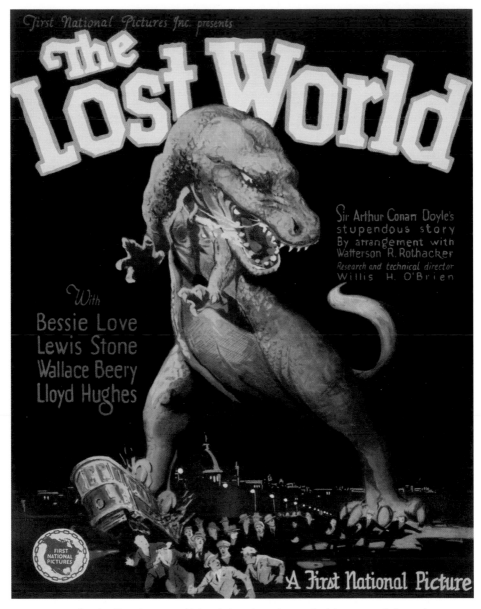

Poster for the film *The Lost World* (1925), based on the novel of the same title by Arthur Conan Doyle. The story tells of a team of scientists and adventurers who find living dinosaurs on a remote plateau in the South American jungle, a motif that would be repeated with variations in countless B-movies and stories in pulp magazines.

Godzilla statue in the Roppongi district, Tokyo. The cinematic monster is fierce yet ultimately benign, a bit like many temple guardians in Asian myth.

Poster for the movie *Godzilla* (1955). This creature combines features of many dinosaurs, including stegosaurus and tyrannosaurus, as well as the Japanese dragon of folklore. It became a model for countless other cinematic dinosaurs and other monsters for decades after the film was released.

the greatest was an ecological collapse, perhaps brought about by climate change, but other scenarios included a deadly pandemic, an invasion from space or a collision of earth with a meteor.

We might effectively destroy ourselves through biotechnology, genetically engineering ourselves out of existence. And, by some understandings at least, extinction may not necessarily be biological. If human culture changes to a point where our basic emotions are unrecognizable, and nobody can begin to understand Shakespeare or Hiroshige, might that count as an extinction? Human identity now seems so ambiguous, and we are becoming so cut off from our past, that one could even wonder if such an extinction has already begun. I will not try to pronounce on how realistic these scenarios are, but fear for our future as human beings is pervasive. Paradoxically, we see ourselves as mighty yet almost endlessly vulnerable, and that is not unlike the way we view the dinosaurs.

Since the early 1980s, it has been widely accepted that the collision of a giant asteroid with earth about 65.5 million years ago in the Yucatan Peninsula finished off the dinosaurs, but their populations had already been under stress and dwindling for millions of years. Many additional theories have been proposed to explain their demise. At the time the asteroid struck, volcanoes known as the Deccan Traps were sending virtual seas of molten rock over much of the earth, which created climatic and further geologic turbulence, and soon led to mass extinctions.[13] Another possible explanation is that the continents became joined through land bridges, allowing populations that had previously been separated to intermingle, thus spreading diseases. Yet another is that species of dinosaurs had become overly specialized, biologically decadent and unable to adapt to new conditions. Or perhaps the dinosaurs died out because early mammals increasingly ate their eggs, preventing them from reproducing in sufficient numbers to continue.

These possibilities are all evocative with respect to the present condition of humankind. If we emphasize the impact of an asteroid, it seems to be a confirmation of Stephen Jay Gould's idea that most things in both nature and human society are not preordained but contingent. If we attribute the demise of the dinosaurs to climate change, that will come across as a warning against ecological complacency. If the reason was the spread of disease due to greater mobility of populations, the caution may be more against globalization, since the continual transport of people and goods from remote parts of the world could help to spread epidemics. It is almost impossible to talk about dinosaurs without saying something about human beings.

Extinction as a metaphor

In the modern era, extinction of a sort increasingly became part of everyday life, as people watched species, cultures, technologies, languages, slang, customs, movements in politics, fashions in dress, styles in art, theories in science and almost everything else appear and then fade into oblivion. Far from being a dramatic apotheosis, this kind of death was the epitome of normal. It left people constantly a bit disoriented, and the culture pervaded by a vague sense of nostalgia, which, in turn, was constantly exploited by commercial interests and generally abhorred by modernists and progressives. One author who artfully captured this nostalgia was Ray Bradbury.

An author of popular science fiction and fantasy, Bradbury often set his stories in the future, perhaps because it seemed fundamentally more stable than the present. This was essentially just a way of updating old romances, and he saw dinosaurs as basically modern dragons. Whatever the time and place, his stories are generally pervaded by a sense of the timelessness of small-town life in the American Midwest around the middle of the twentieth century. Dinosaurs especially appealed to his nostalgia, and he softened the fact of their extinction by making that into part of an eternal condition.

In his story 'The Foghorn', first published in 1951, Bradbury equates the constant obsolescence of institutions in modern life with the extinction of dinosaurs. The lighthouse, which provides ships with a point of orientation by shining a light over the waters, is an institution going back to ancient times. The light was traditionally tended by a keeper, who lived there in solitude, which contrasted with the colourful adventures of mariners in exotic lands. But already, in the mid-twentieth century, lighthouses were gradually being automated, making the keepers unnecessary, just as old cargo ships were replaced by railroads and planes. Other lighthouses were being abandoned and torn down, a trend that was to continue for many decades to come. When the story was first published, the lighthouse, in brief, was on its way to becoming a 'dinosaur'.

'The Foghorn' is set in a lighthouse, where the narrator, Johnny, is staying with the keeper, McDunn. As it grows late, McDunn begins to tell stories, culminating in one of a monster, a dinosaur that has survived millions of years and may be the last of its kind. For the past two years, McDunn explains, the creature has visited the lighthouse every year on the same night, and the date has come around once more. McDunn then turns the foghorn on, a sound that carries 'the sadness of eternity and the briefness of life'. The monster rises from the depths of the sea, answers with a similar call, and walks towards the lighthouse. When McDunn turns the foghorn off, the creature wrecks the lighthouse, and then returns to the sea. The men survive, and a new lighthouse is quickly built, but the creature does not return. When Johnny asks why, McDunn, who often seems to speak for the monster, replies, 'It's gone into the deepest Deeps to wait another million years. Ah, the poor thing! Waiting out there, and waiting out there, while man comes and goes on this pitiful little planet.'[14] Perhaps, in other words, the creature will re-emerge and look for others of its kind, but only after humankind is gone. McDunn and the dinosaur are kindred souls, for both are solitary, anachronistic and able to think in terms of aeons.

About a year later, Bradbury published 'A Sound of Thunder', which is probably the most popular dinosaur tale ever. This time it is the humans who travel through deep time, to visit the realm of our mighty predecessors. The protagonist, Eckels, signs up for a 'time safari', with a company that takes people back into the past for big game hunting, allowing them to bag any creature that they choose. Eckels has chosen a *Tyrannosaurus rex*, the greatest monster ever. The appeal of big game hunting is largely to a sense of power, since you can extinguish the life of a giant. But Travis, his safari guide to the past, quickly makes it clear that Eckels will be anything but powerful. Any change to the past can start a chain of events that will continue over the aeons, so, to avoid changing the future, hunters must obey intricate rules. When scouts have determined that the quarry is nearing the end of its life – in the case of the tyrannosaurus because a tree is about to fall on it – they spray it with red paint to mark it as a target. The hunters can then shoot the creature, but only in the moment when it is already about to die. They may take a photograph of themselves with their 'trophy', but they must leave the body where it fell, and they must never stray onto the grass from an artificial path.

Eckels loses his nerve at the sight of the tyrannosaurus and steps off the path, leaving the guides to shoot it for him. Travis is furious at Eckels and initially wants to leave him stranded in the Mesozoic period, but punishes him by forcing him to retrieve the bullets from the stinking body of the dinosaur instead. On returning to the present, the year 2055, the party members notice many subtle differences. English is spoken a bit differently, and a different candidate has just won the presidential election. Eckels looks at his shoe and finds he has crushed a butterfly, which may have set in motion a series of escalating changes. When Travis realizes what has happened, he raises his gun and shoots Eckels. That shot, and not the roar of *Tyrannosaurus rex*, is, ironically, the 'sound of thunder' referred to in the title.[15]

There are many anomalies in the story. Neither butterflies nor grass had actually evolved in the Age of Dinosaurs. More significantly, the premises of the time safari, at least as explained by Travis, seem entirely arbitrary. The people going back in time must wear oxygen helmets so as not to contaminate the air, and must retrieve their bullets after a kill, yet they do not worry in the least about the red paint left on the dead animal. Travis is distressed that Eckels might have changed the future just by stepping off the path, but, nevertheless, considers leaving his client behind with the dinosaurs. But it is clear that the time safari is a shady business that only manages to survive through graft, so perhaps we are not meant to take its theories about time, and the associated procedures, very seriously. The interpretation of the story that seems most reasonable to me is that every excursion into the past has been altering the present, and dinosaurs, through long sequences of causes and effects, constantly influence our world.

There is a sort of totemic bond between Eckels, representing humankind, and his creaturely antagonist, representing dinosaurs. Both share the combination of apparent dominance with frailty. The man has all the powers of technology yet no freedom, and he is constantly in terror. The dinosaur appears mighty, yet it is about to be killed by a falling tree, and invisible intruders are there to despatch it first. The reason Eckels panics is not physical fear, but that, when looking at the dinosaur, he sees a disconcerting image of himself. In both of these stories by Bradbury, a dinosaur is a sort of alter ego of a man, and the two share a common destiny. In folklore, to meet one's doppelgänger is often a sign of imminent death. McDunn avoids confronting his, and both ultimately survive. Eckels, however, shares the fate of his saurian counterpart.

The last dinosaur

It is odd how dinosaurs vanished from high literature after only a few fragmentary mentions around the middle of the nineteenth century, while becoming the subject of rich and varied stories in fantasy and science fiction, in stories by luminaries such as Ray Bradbury, Isaac Asimov and Arthur C. Clarke. I make no claim for the superiority of either narrative approach, but popular literature was profoundly different from that of the avant-gardes of the nineteenth to mid-twentieth centuries. Popular stories in this period stuck to the traditional conventions of narrative, employing a clear plot that builds to a climax and resolution. They also featured clearly identified narrative strategies, with a relatively unequivocal point of view. Modernist literature experimented with plots, and at times did without them almost entirely, while relating events from multiple or ambiguous points of view. Popular literature, however, generally addressed great cultural and political issues indirectly, while modernists took pride in confronting them in a bold, uncompromising way.

Perhaps the difference comes down to a matter of existential security, resulting in a clear narrative structure, something that popular writers relied on while modernists endeavoured to do without. The popular approach was better suited to dinosaurs, since the associated themes of extinction and immortality were, perhaps, potentially too distressing to be handled any other way. The return of dinosaurs to high literature is, for that reason, a noteworthy event. It comes with the story 'The Dinosaurs' by Italo Calvino in his book *Cosmicomics*, published in the original Italian in 1965 and in English three years later.

Those innovative stories were written out of a feeling that traditional narrative, in spite of all the modernist innovations, was becoming exhausted, since it failed to keep up with developments in science. Calvino did not seek to either popularize science or draw on it, as a science fiction writer, as a source of traditional stories. Rather, he wished to explore the ways in which scientific theories were changing our perception of basic concepts such as space, time and biological identity. Every story began with a scientific topic such as the origin of the cosmos or the appearance of life on land.

The tales in the book are related by a character with the unpronounceable name 'Qfwfq', who has been present at every stage of the earth's history. He is no omniscient narrator but, rather, a vulnerable

participant, and he might be a model for the character of The Doctor in the long-running British television show *Doctor Who*. His ultimate identity is not given, but, as he tells us, he spent about 50 million years as a dinosaur and survived the great extinction. As 'The Dinosaurs' begins, Qfwfq finds himself among the 'new ones' or 'pantotheres', who seem a bit like giant beavers. At first, when the dinosaurs are a memory only several generations removed, Qfwfq looks back on the period with distress at the hardship he experienced, but the new ones think of the dinosaurs with fear. That softens with time, and the terror gives way to nostalgia. Qfwfq himself is partially accepted by the new ones, who do not know what he is. They admire his strength and grant him partial acceptance, yet refer to him as 'the ugly one'. He is befriended by a female named 'Fern-flower', who constantly tells him her dreams of dinosaurs. Those animals of the past are at times fire-breathing monsters, at others melancholy outcasts, and she regards them alternately with horror, pity, admiration and sadism, but none of those stereotypical attitudes rings true to Qfwfq. Eventually the new ones begin to think of the dinosaurs nostalgically and to lament their disappearance, but then they start to forget the primeval lizards entirely.

But the dinosaurs extend their realm by disappearing, ever more deeply, into the thoughts of the new ones and their successors. Qfwfq encounters a 'half breed' who passes through, and mates with her in the bushes. Their child is entirely a dinosaur, yet has no idea what a dinosaur might be. And that is fine with Qfwfq. The dinosaurs, he realizes, can survive best if their identity remains hidden, even from themselves. By that time, he seems to have taken human form, for he takes a train to some metropolis and, as the story ends, is lost in the crowd.[16]

Cover of an issue of the magazine *Amazing Stories*, 1929. This publication was instrumental in establishing the genres of modern pulp fiction, which, like its medieval and early modern predecessors, endeavoured to shock people with the most bizarre events while maintaining a traditional story arc. The insects here, with their spaceship and high-tech weapons, seem like men in space suits, but the tyrannosaurus seems emotionally more human.

Like all the stories in the volume, this one is based on the assumption that identity, whether of an individual or type, is fluid. In what sense has Qfwq been a dinosaur? Do all the millions of years that he has spent as one count as one life or many? These questions are not only unanswered, but, in the context of the stories, they do not even seem important. All literature that is focused on dinosaurs, whether elite or popular, employs a style based on magical realism. Since the subject is mediated by science, it mandates the sort of highly specific detail that we identify with realistic fiction. At the same time, since scientific knowledge is so limited, it is completely pervaded by fantasy. A 'dinosaur' here is not a biological family or a clade, but a sort of eternal type, which was most prevalent in one period of earth's history, yet is not confined to that time. Dinosaur people are perhaps not entirely unlike 'furries', who are anatomically human but prefer to identify as another species such as a wolf or cat. Much as in Bradbury's stories, the dinosaurs live through us, or at least some of us, as human beings.

As the twentieth century gradually drew to a close, there had been increasing concern about the extinction of other species, which could also impact humans by causing an ecological collapse. Scientists now believe we are in the middle of the sixth great extinction in the history of earth. Nobody can say with confidence just how many species are destined for annihilation, but, according to Elizabeth Kolbert, over a third of amphibians, a quarter of all mammals, a fifth of all reptiles and a sixth of birds are probably headed towards oblivion in the decades to come.[17] The hazards are difficult to speak about, and almost impossible to ignore. References to the dinosaurs provide a means of speaking about extinction that is a bit indirect and, thereby, potentially less distressing. Analogies between the two periods of extinction seem especially vivid, because many of the animals facing possible oblivion are ones that are distinguished, like dinosaurs, by their size or ferocity: whales, tigers, elephants, rhinoceroses, pandas, crocodilians, jaguars and so on.

Dinosaurs have been used to embody so many meanings that they are now inseparable from humankind, whether we reflect on them or not. Biological extinction, it appears, is not necessarily the end of evolution, but may be only the beginning. We owe dinosaurs much of our ideas of time, particularly deep time, and many other concepts in human culture. Without them, we might not be fully human. Without us, would they still be dinosaurs? Perhaps human beings might live on, after our apparent extinction, through the computers we have created or through the human genes we have placed in other animals. Perhaps, after 65 or 66 million years of extinction, some 'new ones' may 'resurrect' us, much as we have 'brought back' the dinosaurs in our museum displays and movies. Such possibilities may seem too remote to contemplate, but they are pertinent when we think of our species not as the culmination of evolution up till now but as one, rather fragile, part of the grand panorama of life.

Calvino's story is part of a beginning conversation on the transient nature, not only of individuals, but of species as well. The idea that humanity is not necessarily immortal may ease our collective loneliness, since death is something that all living things have in common. But if we must perish eventually, how would we want to go? What legacy, if any, would we care to leave? Does it matter whether or not our biological line of descent leads to some other species, even if it may not know or care about us in the least? Are the qualities we generally think of as 'human' more intimately associated with the earth or with our DNA?

The late physicist Stephen Hawking believed that humankind has now rendered the earth uninhabitable in the long run, and survival of our species requires colonization of space.[18] Perhaps, at least unconsciously, he is influenced by an analogy with the dinosaurs, a few of which escaped extinction by leaving the land and taking to the air. But, even allowing for the ecological damage being done, I find it difficult to believe that distant planets would be more hospitable to humankind than earth. If they bore relatively little resemblance to earth, we would need to re-engineer almost everything, including the soil and the atmosphere. If they were more like earth, they would carry all sorts of potential diseases and poisons, against which we would have no immunity. Furthermore, leaving earth would only establish a very limited sort of biological continuity between people today and our possible descendants on other planets. Could we really remain 'human' in a broader sense without contact with earth and the many plants and animals that have contributed to human culture?

Part of the reason we so identify with dinosaurs is a deep insecurity, especially with respect to artificial intelligence. The huge dinosaur and the tiny mammal at the end of the Cretaceous era seem a bit like, respectively, a big man and his smartphone. The person might still believe he is in charge, but his mobile phone guides him in many

This 6.5-m-high (21-ft) statue of a torosaurus beside the Peabody Museum in New Haven, Connecticut, was built in 2013 by a team under the direction of the sculptor Michael Anderson. It looks down on the street from a huge base of granite. Around it are replicas of fossil tracks of a therapod, which might have stalked the torosaurus about 66 million years ago.

Sculpture near the entrance to the Fukui Prefectural Dinosaur Museum
in Katsuyama, Japan. Dinosaurs are constantly associated with extinction,
and this figure uses humour to address profound anxiety.

ways, and the person fears that, at least for future generations, it
might take over completely. We call the present the 'Anthropocene'
or 'age of humankind', but it is the start of the 'Digital Age' as well.
What makes us 'human'? We used to think it was intelligence, but now
computers are becoming smarter than people. With respect to technology, we worry constantly about obsolescence or, in other words,
'becoming dinosaurs'.

Illustration by Fernand Besnier to *Le Monde avant la création de l'homme* by Camille Flammarion (1886). All creation going back to the Mesozoic era and before is arranged hierarchically, leading up to Adam and Eve.

CHAPTER VIII

A Dinocentric World

Those masterful images because complete
Grew in pure mind, but out of what began?
A mound of refuse or the sweepings of a street,
Old kettles, old bottles, and a broken can,
Old iron, old bones, old rags, that raving slut
Who keeps the till. Now that my ladder's gone
I must lie down where all the ladders start
In the foul rag and bone shop of the heart.

W. B. YEATS, 'The Circus Animals' Desertion'

Why is the belief in human exceptionalism so persistent in spite of so many indications to the contrary, particularly with respect to evolution? As Stephen Jay Gould has put it, 'Public perception of evolution has been so spin doctored that we have managed to retain an interpretation of human importance scarcely different, in many crucial respects, from the exalted state we occupied as the supposed products of direct creation in God's image.' He refers, of course, to the idea that human beings are the most advanced product in a preordained pattern of evolutionary progress, rather than simply a biological accident.[1] Popular accounts of evolution used to – and, to a large extent, still do – centre all evolutionary developments around

humankind, regarding everything that contributed to man as a step forwards, from the heroic fish that first ventured on land to our upright stance and domestication of fire.

I generally agree with Gould on this point, but the dinosaurs have been an interesting exception to that sort of anthropocentrism. We interpret evolution both before and after the dinosaurs in terms of progress that will culminate in humankind, but the dinosaurs themselves seem more like a very long interruption. If, in fact, we consistently insisted on judging changes over aeons in terms of their contribution to human evolution, the dinosaurs would have to be the great villains of natural history. We would centre our accounts around the diminutive mammals that lived alongside the dinosaurs. We would distinguish sharply among mammalian species of the Mesozoic era, and detail the ways in which they adapted to challenges, while lumping the dinosaurs together as the giants that persecuted them. We might retell the story of the Mesozoic as something like the captivity of the Israelites in Egypt or the contest of David and Goliath, with the mammals as triumphant underdogs. We might write fables about how a primeval rodent outwitted *Tyrannosaurus rex*. We might celebrate the meteor that crashed into earth approximately 65 million years ago, completing the extinction of all non-avian dinosaurs, as a judgment of God or, if we are more secular, as at least a form of mammalian emancipation. It was, after all, what enabled mammals to spread, become more diverse, and eventually evolve into men and women.

That we do not do any of those things shows that, at least on the surface, our narratives of the Mesozoic era are not anthropocentric. They are far more dinocentric. We centre our accounts, in fact, so much around the dinosaurs that the mammals, lizards and

Frontispiece to *The Growing World; or, Progress of Civilization* (1882), published by W. M. Patterson. Starting in the lower-right corner and moving left in a spiral, the picture purports to show a hierarchy of living things, culminating in a cultivated European in the centre. Intruigingly, in this version, insects appear to outrank amphibians and reptiles, perhaps because they live on land and in the air rather than in the water.

crocodilians of their era are often nearly forgotten. If the final extinction of the dinosaurs inspires anything, it is wistful sadness or terror, despite the fact that this is what enabled human beings to live. The reason, I believe, is that dinosaurs have a grandeur that overpowers even our usual inclination towards anthropocentrism.

To understand this paradox, we must first remember that anthropocentrism may take many, seemingly contradictory, forms. It literally means 'centred around man', but what is 'man'? At times people have included great apes but not foreigners or indigenous peoples. Mythology and folklore are full of human–animal composites, such as centaurs or mermaids, and shape-shifters, such as selkies and werewolves, which may or may not count as human. Similarly, we are not sure whether to count Neanderthals or Denisovans as human today. Many people regard their dogs as 'one of the family' and virtually human. As computers duplicate ever more of the abilities once thought exclusive to human beings, science fiction writers and speculative philosophers have wondered if they might eventually attain human status. The meaning of 'human', in summary, is not something that we can take for granted. Biological definitions, in addition to usually being ambiguous, have only a very oblique relationship to the ways in which we usually use the word.

Today, we are thoroughly used to hearing people inveigh against the legacy of anthropocentrism and human exceptionalism. Those who are anatomically 'human' have often been guilty of 'inhuman' behaviour, things such as mass murder or chattel slavery. So why should we care if humankind becomes extinct? To even ask the question might impress some as a little blasphemous, but it is not easy to answer. Fortunately, however, it is also not necessary. We do care,

Illustration by Fernand Besnier to *Le Monde avant la création de l'homme* by Camille Flammarion (1886). In the latter 19th century, many authors blended elements of evolution and creation in colourful, though usually not very systematic, ways. Here, the monkeys looking down at fantastic reptiles of the past represent a sort of 'human' presence, even though they, like people, did not live alongside dinosaurs or plesiosaurs.

Gustave Doré, 'The Creation of the World', from his illustrations to the Bible, 1889.
Note that the artist has borrowed a motif from popular accounts of evolution by
having a creature on the far left, which resembles a dinosaur, crawling out of the sea
to live on land.

even if the cosmos might not. However we may think of people as 'sinners', we still assume that humankind, at almost any price, must be 'saved'. But, whatever 'humanity' may be, our chances of preserving it will be better if we do not commit ourselves to any definition that is too narrow and restrictive. We like to think of qualities such as compassion, emotional complexity and longing for transcendence as 'human', but they may not be exclusively tied to our biology.

We cannot easily decentre humanity in the cosmos, for whatever we place at the centre starts to become 'human'. If we place God at the centre, he is depicted in the image of humankind. If we place animals at the centre, we anthropomorphize them. And what about dinosaurs? Are they human? In many respects, we often seem to think of them in that way. We suggest that by calling a period of millions of years the 'Age of Dinosaurs'. Their size corresponds to our technology, their biological diversity to our cultural variation. Despite being almost unimaginably different from us, dinosaurs are our avatars in the remote past.

No definition of 'humanity' will ever be final or complete, but one way to think about humankind is as the sum of our traditional relationships with other forms of life. Over the centuries, we have developed ways of associating with different animals that are as specific as a biological niche. We want dogs to give us unconditional loyalty and love, and believe they mirror our passions without artifice. Snakes inspire a combination of fear and awe, and are often associated with esoteric knowledge. Deer represent wild nature, and our complex relations with the land are reflected in the ways we both hunt and protect them. Butterflies can represent spirits of the dead, while lions signify kingship. Virtually all animals that have lived alongside human beings for centuries become overlaid with complex, and often antithetical, religious meanings.[2]

Animals are a bit like Catholic saints, at least one of whom is identified with just about every human activity, institution or situation. Our culture has largely been formed through the identification with, and imitation of, animals.[3] In the words of the prominent scholar of human–animal relations Donna Haraway, '*Human* requires an extraordinary congeries of partners. Humans, wherever you track them, are products of situated relationalities with organisms, tools, much else.'[4] Those organisms include dinosaurs. We have not seen much beyond their bones, but we can relate to them across the aeons. They are our guardians of the past and future, the lords of deep time. One reason why the palaeoart of Charles R. Knight or Rudolph Zallinger can resonate long after scientists have declared their models anachronistic is that their paintings are not solely about dinosaurs. They are also about, among other things, the nature of time, the development of life and what it means to be 'human'.

Why dinosaurs?

Most people feel greater kinship with dinosaurs than with the great, prehistoric mammals, more with apatosaurus than with the woolly mammoth and more with tyrannosaurus than with the sabretooth cat. But why? And why specifically with this taxonomic group, dinosaurs, rather than one that might be either larger or smaller? If one wants to be inclusive, why not archosaurs? If one wants to be restrictive, why not just ornithischians or saurischians? Why not sauropods or therapods?

Robert Bakker hoped that public attention might enliven the field of palaeontology and animate our staid image of dinosaurs. Stephen Jay Gould cherished the hope, while realizing that it was often in vain, that young people might initially be drawn by the kitsch but then move on to serious science. But the dinosaur of the palaeontologists has actually never had more than a very tenuous relationship with that of dinomania, which is far closer to being an archetype than a clade. The dinosaur of palaeontology lent an aura of scientific legitimacy to that of dinomania, which, in turn, brought in plenty of funding for museums and research. The two exist in a symbiotic relationship, but they are not, never have been and are never going to be the same.

Scientific terminologies, with their associated conceptual frameworks, are designed for highly specific purposes, and they neither can nor should be adopted for general use. The categories of science can never be internalized in the way that everyday conversation demands. If somebody asks what time it is, he wants an answer in hours and minutes, not in oscillations of the caesium atom. From the viewpoint of cladistics, the word 'fish' may be part of folk taxonomy, but we are not likely to ban it from our conversation on that account. Every clade includes an animal and its descendants, so technically most evolutionary biologists include birds among dinosaurs. But, when they speak of 'dinosaurs' in most contexts, not even scientists are likely to include birds. Dinosaur studies belong in one part of a museum and ornithology in another. As Carol Kaesuk Yoon has put this, 'Even if we always only heard and saw newfangled terms for evolutionarily sensible groupings, such a vision of life would still, as it does now, seem foreign.'[5]

Classification is not a matter of fact but of convenience and analysis. Every system of classification is an interpretation of experience, with implicit assumptions. What is a human being? As already indicated, nobody knows for sure. And what is a dinosaur? Personally, I think 'big, fierce, and extinct' may be as good a definition as any. Yoon has proposed that, rather than trying to standardize the classification of living things by imposing a single model, we open ourselves to a wide range of taxonomies. If we present a single one such as cladistics, the system currently favoured by biologists, as exclusively correct, we not only limit our imaginations. We also, since the taxonomies are so abstract, increasingly separate ourselves from the sensuous manifestations of the natural world.

People have many conceptions of immortality, and some speak of living on through their soul, their deeds, their writing or their memory. Cladistics has a version of immortality, which is through a line of descent. An animal is defined by its ancestry, so birds are still dinosaurs and human beings are apes. An animal is regarded as extinct only if its line dies out. This is basically a religious idea, and it is not one that will satisfy everybody. Tiktaalik, the fishlike animal that scientists believe first colonized the land, has produced a vast range and number of evolutionary progeny, but it is not still with us today.

The definition of kinship in cladistics here is extremely narrow, and it does not take into account most of the ways in which this is generally understood. We do not necessarily feel the strongest sense of kinship with blood relatives; in fact we may very well feel more with our spouses and even friends. We are also likely to feel more kinship with dogs, which excel at reading human emotions, than with chimpanzees. Many people feel an intense, and highly personal, kinship, in the sense of identification, with specific varieties of animal, which may be anything from butterflies to turtles.

Yoon is willing to accept the seemingly paradoxical implications of her approach. In her words, 'To really reclaim the human umwelt (i.e., perceptual environment) . . . we will need to wrap our minds around more than whales as fish. We will need to welcome in all manner of wondrous absurd-seeming possibilities: cassowaries as mammals, orchids as thumbs, and bats as birds.'[6] By exclusively classifying creatures in terms of biological descent rather than physical, behavioural, geographic or psychological characteristics, we remove them from sensual experience. We then compensate for the lack of vividness by the heavy use of electronic gimmickry, overwhelming individual creativity with a manufactured fantasy. By opening ourselves to several taxonomies, and the analytic frameworks that accompany them, we also open ourselves to a reality that is greater than any of them alone.

Many living things that are not closely related biologically develop similar characteristics through convergence. Bats and butterflies move through the air like birds. Many salamanders shoot out their tongues further than the length of their bodies to catch insects, much like chameleons. Other animals develop similar characteristics through mimicry. The viceroy butterfly has much the same pattern on its wings as the monarch, developed to fool potential predators into thinking

Gustave Doré, 'Monsters in Astolfo's Path', illustration to *Orlando furioso* by Ludovico Ariosto, 1877. Already, in the latter 19th century, the discovery of dinosaurs had influenced the ways in which people imagined monsters. The creature on the far left, especially, could easily be an apatosaurus or another sauropod.

that, like the monarch butterfly, it contains toxic chemicals. Finally, different species can develop similar characteristics through close interaction, such as the ways of expressing emotion in dogs and human beings.

Perhaps humanity might be better understood more as a set of relationships, an ecological and historical niche, than as a strand of

DNA. These include relations not only with creatures alive today but with those of the future and the past. Our interaction with dinosaurs takes place across a span of several million years, and it is not reciprocal. We know them mostly through their huge bones, but we have, nevertheless, imagined them as dragons, deities and demons. We may perhaps have mimicked their features in our masks, and empathized with them in legends. We may have developed abilities that are parallel to theirs. In many senses, they might even be our 'next of kin'.

Scientists began to name and describe dinosaurs round the beginning of the modern era, almost the same time as people, or at least the Euro-American intelligentsia, had largely ceased to believe in dragons. Because of this, dinosaurs seemed to be an entirely new 'discovery', rather than a refinement of dragon lore. Early researchers obscured the continuity between dragons and dinosaurs as well as, more broadly, that between myth and science. As heroes from Cadmus to St George would slay dragons to usher in the modern age, so those of pulp fiction and video games often kill dinosaurs. The two sorts of creature have blended, once again, in popular culture.

Maybe, for some purposes at least, we should regard dinosaurs as big and fierce but not necessarily extinct. To make sense of phenomena like dinomania, we need to understand 'dinosaur' broadly as a construction in which palaeontologists are not the sole arbiters. This is simply recognizing a state of affairs that has already long prevailed, perhaps since the Crystal Palace Park. No definition of 'dinosaur' will ever be satisfactory in every context, but we need to consider ways of understanding dinosaurs not just in terms of biology but also ecology, tradition and our collective imagination.

This is similar to recent developments in cryptozoology. Until recently, that was a marginal discipline, which focused heavily on investigating the existence of half-legendary animals such as the yeti or the great sea serpent. Certainly, the yeti exists in some form, whether it is as a hominid, bear, monkey, hallucination or something else entirely. Cultures other than the modern West may regard it in

Jan Sovak, *Torvosaurus and Brachiosaurus, c.* 2006. Most palaeoartists still emphasize the profound otherness of dinosaurs. This picture, however, adds a sort of 'human' touch.

DON'T DISTURB THE DINOSAURS

Sixty-million years too late! All that's left are the bones of these gigantic reptiles. But what an amazing world of the past they bring to light. Behold their fossilized remains embedded in one of the world's largest graveyards at Dinosaur National Monument in Utah. See other prehistoric artifacts on display at the Natural History State Park in Vernal.

The ageless past is revealed not only in Dinosaurland but throughout the different world of Utah. There are fantastic erosions, awesome gorges, vast volcanic regions, ancient Indian ruins and petroglyphs, and the huge salty remnant of a 100,000 year old lake. Not so ancient, historic Mormon architecture from early log cabins to massive temples and tabernacles; countless museums and exhibits that display treasured heirlooms from Utah's pioneer past; Indian celebrations, fairs and dances that recall a vanishing primitive life.

Fishing at Utah's Flaming Gorge is unbelievably good.

Ute Indians in Dinosaurland hold annual dances.

Mail this coupon today for your FREE Utah Travel Kit: full-color Utah booklet; complete fact book on attractions, events, accommodations, rates; and highway map.

UTAH TRAVEL COUNCIL, DEPT. 116
COUNCIL HALL • CAPITOL HILL
SALT LAKE CITY, UTAH 84114

NAME ....

ADDRESS ....

CITY .... STATE .... ZIP ....
A visit to Utah is second best only to living and investing in Utah.

Discover the Different World of

UTAH!

Advertisement promoting tourism in the state of Utah, *c.* 1960. Dinosaurs, together with Native Americans, are portrayed as part of an idealized past where all things are contemporaneous.

terms of ontologies that are hard for us to comprehend. They might not distinguish as sharply, or in the same way as we, between a human being and a monkey or bear. They might even have alternative ways of thinking of time, space and consciousness. But the status and origin of the yeti is only one aspect of its legend, and not always the most subtle or interesting. By cultivating an openness to a wider range of questions and ontologies, cryptozoologists have revitalized, and brought new status to, their field.[7]

I have previously discussed how a very substantial segment of the American public believes that dinosaurs and people lived at the same time. This represents, without any doubt, a very serious failure of American education. But the way to correct this is not, in my opinion, to persuade or compel people to think about dinosaurs in cladistic terms all the time. Rather, it is to empower them to distinguish between various ontologies. They will then be able to appreciate that dinosaurs were not contemporaries of people in the most literal sense, but might be in others that are just as genuine. As also noted, almost everyone who is interested in dinosaurs seems to fantasize about meeting them in one way or another. Perhaps they can satisfy this desire without indulging in falsehoods.

Palaeontologists should not be high priests of dinomania. They ought to retain a place of special honour, but they should share it with artists, writers, philosophers and general dinosaur enthusiasts, all of whom endeavour to place dinosaurs in cultural and intellectual contexts. This would mean that scientists could not so easily transfer their authority to commercial interests, and it would, I believe, liberate the dinosaurs from some of the kitsch that has, for over a century and a half, surrounded them. Museum shops might even devote slightly less space to dinosaur toys and include literature by authors such as Ray Bradbury and Italo Calvino.

People without dinosaurs

How did dinosaurs appear? To even consider the question, we need to project ourselves back in time, as a sort of hypothetical observer. For that reason, even the most informed descriptions or pictorial representations of dinosaurs involve an element of science fiction. We would not be adapted to the environment, and so there is very little we can take for granted. How might our senses be affected by the climate and atmosphere? How might we respond psychologically to such a world? The objective of describing dinosaurs is a radical challenge to the human imagination. Perhaps all our reconstructions are mostly fantasy, and the scientific foundation is in large part a device to facilitate suspension of disbelief.

As a thought experiment, let us imagine a world without dinosaurs. Let us say that they had never existed, so early mammals (which actually appeared on earth at about the same time as dinosaurs or even a

Dinosaur Village in Chiang Mai, Thailand. Dinosaurs play a unique role in contemporary culture, poised between fantasy and science.

Painting by Carl Buell, *c.* 2012. The blue dinosaur in the foreground is *Obamadon gracilis*, named in 2008 after the 44th president of the United States. It looks on thoughtfully as predators pursue and struggle with their prey, and an asteroid, which may destroy them all, approaches earth in the background.

bit earlier) had little competition. In consequence, human beings developed about 170 million years earlier. Since this is all fantasy in any case, let us suppose that human culture had still developed following our pattern, with books, art, science and technology. The only thing that is radically different is that, when scientists reconstruct the remote past, there are no dinosaurs. Under such circumstances, I imagine that human arrogance would be even more extreme than now, for it would seem far easier to imagine ourselves the culmination of evolutionary history.

While we are at it, let us, alternatively, imagine a world without mammals. Suppose that dinosaurs had not become extinct, and human beings were their direct descendants. After all, dinosaurs were largely bipedal and may have had warm blood. My guess is that the theory of evolution would have encountered far less resistance. After all, the proverbial monkey for a grandfather might be okay, but a dinosaur for a grandfather would be more impressive. People, in fact, would be wondering how the dinosaurs had 'degenerated' to become human. Scientists might argue about which dinosaur man was descended from. Those who claimed a *Tyrannosaurus rex* as an ancestor might even be accused of excessive human pride.

Finally, let us try to imagine a world without humans of any sort, whether mammalian, reptilian or avian. Suppose that dinosaurs, along with other forms of life, had simply continued to evolve for another 65 million years and more, constantly generating new forms of life, yet none with a great resemblance to human beings or their civilization. We would then be one more unrealized potential, a sort of 'might have been', not entirely unlike what a mature man envisages when he contemplates what would have happened had he chosen a different career.

Yes, this is make-believe. My tone is a little humorous, but fantasy is a legitimate way in which we try to come to terms with our fate as human beings. These scenarios are thought experiments, intended to expand our imaginations and perhaps clarify our values. Dinosaurs inspire us to imagine new worlds and explore new possibilities. What I think these daydreams of alternative evolution show is that dinosaurs are an essential part of the way we construct our identity as human beings. Of all the animals that evolution has produced, they are the ones that perhaps provide the closest parallel to humankind. We might even say that 'humankind is a dinosaur', with all the fears, endowments and ambiguities that entails.

Science, in my opinion, is indeed driven by a sense of wonder, but it constantly exhausts that feeling, which must then be replenished by new discoveries. Wonder comes in moments of recognition, when the old analytical frameworks are stripped away, revealing a reality that is far more vast and complex than the researcher had usually assumed. Wonder is diminished as we replace the old theories with new ones, limiting possibilities and returning to staid routines. It requires constant innovation and is not encouraged, at least not for long, by contemplating the intricate theoretical structures that we have built around fairly simple experiences. To remain vital, science must continually return to its source, and in dinosaur studies that is primeval bones.

I have documented in this book how dinosaurs have been, increasingly since their discovery, perpetually surrounded by kitsch, but I do not dwell on this to encourage feelings of superiority. This is not a criticism of dinosaurs, nor is it simply a disparagement of the institutions that have grown up about them. I freely admit to enjoying dinosaur kitsch in moderation, though nowadays it far exceeds my level of comfort. But I have mentioned this because it seems necessary to work our way through all the commercial hype to arrive at something genuine. My standard is still my earliest encounter with a dinosaur exhibit in a museum, which remains the simplest — the huge dinosaur bone in Chicago's Field Museum, which was displayed, with no fanfare whatsoever, for visitors to touch.

REFERENCES

1 Dragon Bones

1 Gail F. Melson, *Why the Wild Things Are: Animals in the Lives of Children* (Cambridge, MA, 2001), p. 152.
2 Tom Rea, *Bone Wars: The Excavation and Celebrity of Andrew Carnegie's Dinosaur* (Pittsburgh, PA, 2001), p. 8.
3 Martin J. S. Rudwick, *Scenes from Deep Time: Early Pictorial Representations of the Prehistoric World* (Chicago, IL, 1992), p. 237.
4 Adrienne Mayor, *The First Fossil Hunters: Paleontology in Greek and Roman Times* (Princeton, NJ, 2000), pp. 177–8.
5 Judy Allen and Jeanne Griffiths, *The Book of the Dragon* (Secaucus, NJ, 1979), p. 90.
6 Mayor, *Fossil Hunters*, pp. 15–53.
7 Ibid., pp. 195–202.
8 Allen and Griffiths, *Book of the Dragon*, p. 36.
9 Pranay Lal, 'The Fascinating History of When Rajasaurus and Other Dinosaurs Roamed the Indian Subcontinent', https://qz.com/866159, accessed 4 July 2017.
10 Herodotus, *The Histories*, trans. Peter B. Willberg (New York, 1997), pp. 37–8.
11 Harold Gebhardt and Mario Ludwig, *Von Drachen, Yetis und Vampiren: Fabeltieren auf der Spur* (Munich, 2000), p. 202.
12 Willy Ley, *Dawn of Zoology* (New York, 1968), p. 193.
13 Gebhardt and Ludwig, *Von Drachen*, p. 203.
14 Ibid., p. 42.
15 Ibid., p. 205.

16 R. H. Marijnissin and P. Ruyffelaere, *Bosch: The Complete Works* (Antwerp, 1987), pp. 134–53.

17 Suzanne Boorsch, 'The 1688 Paradise Lost and Dr Aldrich', *Metropolitan Museum Journal*, VI (1972), pp. 133–50.

18 Georges Louis Leclerc, Comte de Buffon, *Les Époques de la nature*, vol. II (Paris, 1780), pp. 126–36.

19 Johann Jakob Scheuchzer, *Homo diluvii testis* (Zurich, 1726)

20 Herbert Wendt, *In Search of Adam: The Story of Man's Quest for the Truth about His Earliest Ancestors* (New York, 1956), p. 15.

21 Ibid., p. 16.

22 Helen Macdonald, 'A Bestiary of the Mind', *New York Times Magazine*, 21 May 2017, pp. 40–41.

11 How Dragons Became Dinosaurs

1 David D. Gilmore, *Monsters: Evil Beings, Mythical Beasts, and All Manner of Imaginary Terrors* (Philadelphia, PA, 2003), p. 73.

2 David Leeming and Margaret Leeming, *A Dictionary of Creation Myths* (Oxford, 1994), pp. 202–8.

3 Hesiod, *Theogony/Works and Days* [750 BCE], trans. M. L. West (Oxford, 1988), pp. 3–33.

4 Alan Weller, ed., *120 Visions of Heaven and Hell* (Mineola, NY, 2010), pl. 064.

5 William Shakespeare, *Shakespeare's Sonnets*, ed. Margaret de Grazia (New York, 2011), p. 157.

6 John Milton, *Paradise Lost* [1667–74] (Oxford, 2003), book X.

7 Thomas Hawkins, *The Book of the Great Sea-dragons, Ichthyosauri and Plesiosauri* (London, 1840), p. 21.

8 Deborah Cadbury, *The Dinosaur Hunters: A Story of Scientific Rivalry and the Discovery of the Prehistoric World* (New York, 2001), pp. 141–2.

9 Isabella Duncan, *Pre-Adamite Man; or, the Story of Our Old Planet and Its Inhabitants, Told by Scripture and Science* (London, 1861).

10 Joscelyn Godwin, *Athanasius Kircher: A Renaissance Man and the Quest for Lost Knowledge* (London, 1979), pp. 25–33, 84–93.

11 Thomas Burnet, *The Sacred Theory of the Earth* [1690] (London, 1816), p. 29.

12 Edmund Burke, *A Philosophical Enquiry Into the Origin of Our Ideas of the Sublime and Beautiful* [1757] (Oxford, 2015), pp. 47–9.

13 Donald Worster, *Nature's Economy: A History of Ecological Ideas* (Cambridge, MA, 1994), p. 125.

III Mister Big and Mister Fierce

1 William Paley, *Natural Theology*, facsimile edition (Boston, MA, 1841), p. 265.
2 Ibid.
3 William Smellie, *The Philosophy of Natural History*, 5th edn (Boston, MA, 1838), p. 222.
4 Deborah Cadbury, *The Dinosaur Hunters: A Story of Scientific Rivalry and the Discovery of the Prehistoric World* (New York, 2001), p. 95.
5 Gideon Mantell, 'The Age of Reptiles', *The Star*, 16 June 1831, p. 1.
6 George F. Richardson, *Sketches in Prose and Verse (second series), containing visits to the Mantellian Museum* (London, 1838).
7 Martin J. S. Rudwick, *Scenes of Deep Time: Early Representations of the Primitive World* (Chicago, IL, 1992), p. 119.
8 David Hone, *The Tyrannosaur Chronicles: The Biology of the Tyrant Dinosaurs* (New York, 2016), p. 21.
9 Mark A. Norell et al., *Discovering Dinosaurs in the American Museum of Natural History* (New York, 1995), pp. 105–6.
10 Stephen Jay Gould, 'Dinomania', in *Dinosaur in a Haystack: Reflections on Natural History* (New York, 1995), p. 223.
11 David D. Gilmore, *Monsters: Evil Beings, Mythical Beasts, and All Manner of Imaginary Terrors* (Philadelphia, PA, 2003), p. 72.
12 Alan A. Debus, *Dinosaurs in Fantastic Fiction: A Thematic Survey* (London, 2006), p. 125.
13 http://books.google.com/ngrams.
14 Paul A. Trout, *Deadly Powers: Animal Predators and the Mythic Imagination* (Amherst, NY, 2011), p. 21.

IV From the Crystal Palace to Jurassic Park

1 Peter Marshall, *The Magic Circle of Rudolf II: Alchemy and Astrology in Renaissance Prague* (New York, 2006), p. 76.
2 Deborah Cadbury, *The Dinosaur Hunters: A Story of Scientific Rivalry and the Discovery of the Prehistoric World* (London, 2001), pp. 211, 216–17.
3 David D. Gilmore, *Monsters: Evil Beings, Mythical Beasts and All Manner of Imaginary Terrors* (Philadelphia, PA, 2003), pp. 62–3.
4 Celeste Olalquiaga, *The Artificial Kingdom: A Treasury of Kitsch Experience* (New York, 1998), p. 32.
5 Ibid.

6 Steve McCarthy and Mick Gilbert, *The Crystal Palace Dinosaurs* (London, 1994), p. 31.

7 Ibid., p. 67.

8 W.J.T. Mitchell, *The Last Dinosaur Book: The Life and Times of a Cultural Icon* (Chicago, IL, 1998), p. 128.

9 Douglas J. Preston, *Dinosaurs in the Attic: An Excursion into the American Museum of Natural History* (New York, 1993), p. 25.

10 Henry Neville Hutchinson and William Henry Flower, *Creatures of Other Days* (London, 1894), p. 142.

11 McCarthy and Gilbert, *The Crystal Palace Dinosaurs*, p. 41.

12 Brian Switek, 'Darwin and the Dinosaurs', www.smithsonian.com, 12 February 2009.

13 Preston, *Dinosaurs*, pp. 78–9.

14 Tom Rea, *Bone Wars: The Excavation and Celebrity of Andrew Carnegie's Dinosaur* (Pittsburgh, PA, 2001), p. 31.

15 Ibid., p. 41.

16 Ibid., pp. 42–3.

17 Ibid., p. 164.

18 Zoë Lescaze, *Paleoart: Visions of the Prehistoric Past* (New York, 2017), pp. 216–64.

19 Anonymous, *The Exciting World of Dinosaurs: Sinclair Dinoland* (New York, 1964), n.p.

20 Anonymous, 'Dinos Popular', *Simpson's Leader-Times*, 19 August 1965, p. 14.

21 Asher Elbein, 'The Right's Dinosaur Fetish: Why the Koch Brothers are Obsessed with Paleontology', www.salon.com, 28 July 2014.

22 Joe Cunningham, 'Behind the Scenes at Dinomania', *Syracuse New Times*, www.syracusenewtimes.com, 15 October 2014.

23 Stephen J. Gould, 'The Dinosaur Rip-off', in *Bully for Brontosaurus: Reflections on Natural History* (New York, 1991), p. 98.

24 Mitchell, *The Last Dinosaur Book*, p. 14.

25 Bruno Latour, *We Have Never Been Modern*, trans. Catherine Porter (Cambridge, MA, 1993), p. 21.

v The Dinosaur Renaissance

1 Thomas S. Kuhn, *The Structure of Scientific Revolutions*, 2nd edn (Chicago, IL, 1962).

2 Robert Bakker, 'The Superiority of Dinosaurs', *Discovery*, III/2 (1968), pp. 11–22.

3 Robert Bakker, *Dinosaur Heresies: New Theories Unlocking the Mystery of the Dinosaurs and Their Extinction* (New York, 1986), pp. 1–19.
4 David Norman, *Dinosaur* (New York, 1991), p. 69.
5 Zoë Lescaze, *Paleoart: Visions of the Prehistoric Past* (New York, 2017), pp. 111–14.
6 Jane P. Davidson, *A History of Paleontology Illustration* (Bloomington, IN, 2008), pp. 169–72.
7 John Noble Wilford, *The Riddle of the Dinosaurs* (New York, 1985), pp. 161–75.
8 W.J.T. Mitchell, *The Last Dinosaur Book* (Chicago, IL, 1980), p. 64.
9 Niles Eldredge and Stephen J. Gould, 'Punctuated Equilibria. An Alternative to Phyletic Gradualism', in *Models in Paleobiology*, ed. T.J.M. Schropf (Cambridge, 1972), p. 86.
10 Derek Turner, *Paleontology: A Philosophical Introduction* (Cambridge, 2011), pp. 51–71.
11 Martin J. S. Rudwick, *Earth's Deep History: How It Was Discovered and Why It Matters* (Chicago, IL, 2014), p. 263.
12 Darren Naish and Paul Barrett, *Dinosaurs: How They Lived and Evolved* (Washington, DC, 2016), p. 24.
13 Lescaze, *Paleoart*, pp. 268, 272–7.
14 Davidson, *A History of Paleontology Illustration*, pp. 153–6, 173, 180.
15 Lescaze, *Paleoart*, p. 268.

VI The Totem of Modernity

1 Mircea Eliade, *The Myth of the Eternal Return* (Princeton, NJ, 1974), pp. 139–64.
2 Allen A. Debus, *Dinosaurs in Fantastic Fiction: A Thematic Survey* (London, 2011), pp. 36–55, 85–102.
3 Stephen T. Asma, *Stuffed Animals and Pickled Heads: The Culture and Evolution of Natural History Museums* (Oxford, 2001), p. 155.
4 Samuel Philips, *Guide to the Crystal Palace and Park: Facsimile Edition of 1856 Official Guide* (London, 2008), p. 193.
5 Philip Henry Gosse, *The Romance of Natural History* (London, 1860), pp. 330–40.
6 J. P. O'Neill, *The Great New England Sea Serpent: An Account of Unknown Creatures Sighted by Many Respectable Persons between 1638 and the Present Day* (Camden, ME, 1999), pp. 112, 147.
7 Debus, *Dinosaurs in Fantastic Fiction*, p. 39.

8 David D. Gilmore, *Monsters: Evil Beings, Mythical Beasts, and All Manner of Imaginary Terrors* (Philadelphia, PA, 2002), pp. 2, 192.

9 Jack Horner and James Gorman, *How to Build a Dinosaur: The New Science of Reverse Evolution* (New York, 2010).

10 W.J.T. Mitchell, *The Last Dinosaur Book: The Life and Times of a Cultural Icon* (Chicago, IL, 1998), p. 91.

11 Ibid., pp. 77 85.

12 Ibid., p. 77.

13 Claude Lévi-Strauss, *The Savage Mind*, trans. anon. (Chicago, IL, 1966), pp. 232–3.

14 Bruno Latour, *We Have Never Been Modern*, trans. Catherine Porter (Cambridge, MA, 1993), p. 91.

15 Ibid., p. 84.

16 Ibid.

17 Jean-François Lyotard, *The Postmodern Condition: A Report on Knowledge*, trans. Geoff Bennington and Brian Massumi (Minneapolis, MN, 1979), pp. 31–41.

18 Latour, *We Have Never Been Modern*, p. 21.

19 Philippe Descola, *Beyond Nature and Culture*, trans. Janet Lloyd (Chicago, IL, 2005), pp. 144–71.

20 Marshall Sahlins, *What Kinship Is and Is Not* (Chicago, IL, 2013), p. 7.

21 Harold Gebhardt and Maria Ludwig, *Von Drachen, Yetis und Vampiren: Fabeltieren auf der Spur* (Munich, 2005), p. 41.

VII Extinction

1 Stephen J. Gould, 'The Dinosaur Rip-off', in *Bully for Brontosaurus: Reflections on Natural History* (New York, 1991), p. 96.

2 Gail F. Melson, *Why the Wild Things Are: Animals in the Lives of Children* (Cambridge, MA, 2001), pp. 62–4.

3 Willy Ley, *Dawn of Zoology* (New York, 1968), p. 203.

4 Georges Cuvier, *Georges Cuvier, Fossil Bones and Geological Catastrophes: New Translations and Interpretations of the Primary Texts*, ed. Martin J. S. Rudwick (Chicago, IL, 1997), pp. 186–7.

5 Rev. J. G. Wood, *Animate Creation*, vol. I (New York, 1885), p. 9.

6 Martin J. S. Rudwick, *Scenes from Deep Time: Early Pictorial Representations of the Prehistoric World* (Chicago, IL, 1992), pp. 48–50.

7 Alfred, Lord Tennyson, 'In Memoriam', in *Selected Poems* (New York, 1993), pp. 137–8.

8 Steve McCarthy and Mick Gilbert, *The Crystal Palace Dinosaurs: The Story of the World's First Prehistoric Sculptures* (London, 1994), p. 22. The grammar used in the song has been adjusted a bit, to bring it in line with current usage.

9 Charles Dickens, *Bleak House* [1852–3] (New York, 2004), p. 13.

10 Joe Zammit-Lucia, 'Practice and Ethics of the Use of Animals in Contemporary Art', in *The Oxford Handbook of Animal Studies*, ed. Linda Kalof (Oxford, 2017), pp. 444–5.

11 W.J.T. Mitchell, *The Last Dinosaur Book: The Life and Times of a Cultural Icon* (Chicago, IL, 1998), p. 62.

12 Ibid., pp. 265–75.

13 Peter Ward and Joe Kirschvink, *A New History of Life: The Radical New Discoveries about the Origins and Evolution of Life on Earth* (New York, 2015), pp. 296–306.

14 Ray Bradbury, 'The Foghorn', in *Dinosaur Tales* (New York, 1925), pp. 94–111.

15 Ray Bradbury, 'A Sound of Thunder', in *Dinosaur Tales* (New York, 1925), pp. 51–86.

16 Italo Calvino, 'The Dinosaurs', in *The Complete Cosmicomics*, trans. Martin McLaughlin (New York, 2015), pp. 99–113.

17 Elizabeth Kolbert, *The Sixth Extinction: An Unnatural History* (New York, 2014), p. 21.

18 Peter Holley, 'Stephen Hawking Now Says that Humanity Has Only About 100 Years to Escape Earth', www.chicagotribune.com, 8 May 2017.

VIII A Dinocentric World

1 Stephen Jay Gould, 'Can We Complete Darwin's Revolution?', in *Dinosaur in a Haystack: Reflections on Natural History* (New York, 1995), pp. 326–7.

2 Boria Sax, *The Mythical Zoo: Animals in Myth, Legend and Literature*, 2nd edn (New York and London, 2013), pp. 13–16, 331–2.

3 Paul Shepard, *The Others: How Animals Made Us Human* (Washington, DC, 1966), pp. 13–27.

4 Nicholas Gane and Donna Haraway, 'Interview with Donna Haraway', *Theory, Culture and Society* (2006), XXIII/7–8, p. 146.

5 Carol Kaesuk Yoon, *Naming Nature: The Clash Between Instinct and Science* (New York, 2009), p. 230.

6 Ibid., p. 235.

7 Samantha Hurn, 'Introduction', in *Anthropology and Cryptozoology: Exploring Encounters with Mysterious Creatures*, ed. Samantha Hurn (London, 2017), pp. 1–12.

BIBLIOGRAPHY

Note: This list is intended primarily to provide suggestions for further reading and is aimed more at the general reader than the specialist. For this reason, I have not included all the works cited in the References.

Adler, Alan, ed., *Science-fiction and Horror Movie Posters in Full Color* (Mineola, NY, 1977)

Asma, Stephen T., *Stuffed Animals and Pickled Heads: The Culture and Evolution of Natural History Museums* (Oxford, 2001)

Bakker, Robert T., *The Dinosaur Heresies: New Theories Unlocking the Mystery of the Dinosaurs and Their Extinction* (New York, 1986)

Boorsch, Suzanne, 'The 1688 Paradise Lost and Dr. Aldrich', *Metropolitan Museum Journal*, VI (1972), pp. 133–50

Bradbury, Ray, *Dinosaur Tales* (New York, 2003)

Burke, Edmund, *A Philosophical Inquiry into the Sublime and the Beautiful* [1757] (Oxford, 2009)

Cadbury, Deborah, *The Dinosaur Hunters: A Story of Scientific Rivalry and the Discovery of the Prehistoric World* (London, 2001)

Calvino, Italo, *The Complete Cosmicomics,* trans. Martin McLaughlin (New York, 2015)

Crichton, Michael, *Jurassic Park* (New York, 1990)

—, *The Lost World* (New York, 1995)

Cuvier, Georges, *Fossil Bones and Geological Catastrophes*, trans. Martin J. S. Rudwick (Chicago, IL, 1997)

Davidson, Jane P., *A History of Paleontological Illustration* (Bloomington, IN, 2008)

Debus, Allen A., *Dinosaurs in Fantastic Fiction* (Jefferson, NC, 2006)

Dickens, Charles, *Bleak House* [1853–4] (New York, 2004)

Doyle, Arthur Conan, *The Lost World* [1912] (Toronto, 2015)

Eliade, Mircea, *The Myth of the Eternal Return* (Princeton, NJ, 1974)

Gebhardt, Harold and Mario Ludwig, *Von Drachen, Yetis und Vampiren: Fabeltieren auf der Spur* (Munich, 2005)

Gilmore, David D., *Monsters: Evil Beings, Mythical Beasts, and All Manner of Imaginary Terrors* (Philadelphia, PA, 2003)

Gould, Stephen Jay, *Bully for Brontosaurus: Reflections on Natural History* (New York, 1991)

—, *Dinosaur in a Haystack* (New York, 1995)

—, *Time's Arrow, Time's Cycle: Myth and Metaphor in the Discovery of Geological Time* (Cambridge, MA, 1987)

Gould, Stephen J., and Niles Eldredge, 'Punctuated Equilibria: An Alternative to Phyletic Gradualism', in *Models in Paleobiology*, ed. T.J.M. Schropf (San Francisco, CA, 1972), pp. 82–115

Greenberg, Martin H., ed., *Dinosaurs* (New York, 1996)

Herodotus, *The Histories*, trans. Peter B. Willberg [c. 420 BCE] (New York, 1997)

Hone, David, *The Tyrannosaur Chronicles: The Biology of Tyrant Dinosaurs* (New York, 2016)

Horner, Jack, and James Gorman, *How to Build a Dinosaur: The New Science of Reverse Evolution* (New York, 2010)

Hurn, Samantha, ed., *Anthropology and Cryptozoology: Exploring Encounters with Mysterious Creatures* (Abingdon, 2017)

Kolbert, Elizabeth, *The Sixth Extinction: An Unnatural History* (New York, 2014)

Kuhn, Thomas S., *The Structure of Scientific Revolutions*, 2nd edn (Chicago, IL, 1970)

Larson, Edward J., *Evolution: A Remarkable History of a Scientific Theory* (New York, 2004)

Latour, Bruno, *Politics of Nature: How to Bring the Sciences into Democracy*, trans. Catherine Porter (Cambridge, MA, 2004)

—, *We Have Never Been Modern*, trans. Catherine Porter (Cambridge, MA, 1993)

Leeming, David, and Margaret Leeming, *A Dictionary of Creation Myths* (Oxford, 1994)

Lescaze, Zoë, and Walton Ford, *Paleoart: Visions of the Prehistoric Past, 1830–1980* (New York, 2017)

Lévi-Strauss, Claude, *The Savage Mind*, no translator given (Chicago, IL, 1966)

Ley, Willy, *The Dawn of Zoology* (Englewood Cliffs, NJ, 1968)

Lyotard, Jean-François, *The Postmodern Condition: A Report on Knowledge*, trans. Brian Massumi (Minneapolis, MN, 1984)

Mayor, Adrienne, *The First Fossil Hunters: Paleontology in Greek and Roman Times* (Princeton, NJ, 2000)

Melson, Gail F., *Why the Wild Things Are: Animals in the Lives of Children* (Cambridge, MA, 2001)

Mitchell, W.J.T., *The Last Dinosaur Book: The Life and Times of a Cultural Icon* (Chicago, IL, 1998)

Naish, Darren, and Paul Barrett, *Dinosaurs: How They Lived and Evolved* (Washington, DC, 2016)

Norman, David, *Dinosaur* (New York, 1991)

—, *Dinosaurs* (Oxford, 2005)

Olalquiaga, Celeste, *The Artificial Kingdom: A Treasury of Kitsch Experience* (New York, 1998)

Preston, Douglas J., *Dinosaurs in the Attic: An Excursion into the American Museum of Natural History* (New York, 1993)

Rea, Tom, *Bone Wars: The Excavation and Celebrity of Andrew Carnegie's Dinosaur* (Pittsburgh, PA, 2001)

Rudwick, Martin J. S., *Earth's Deep History: How It Was Discovered and Why It Matters* (Chicago, IL, 2014)

—, *Scenes from Deep Time: Early Pictorial Representations of the Prehistoric World* (Chicago, IL, 1992)

Sanz, José Luis, *Starring T. Rex! Dinosaur Mythology in Popular Culture*, trans. Philip Mason (Bloomington, IN, 2002)

Sax, Boria, *The Mythical Zoo: Animals in Myth, Legend and Literature*, 2nd edn (New York, 2013)

Shepard, Paul, *The Others: How Animals Made Us Human* (Washington, DC, 1996)

Trout, Paul A., *Deadly Powers: Animal Predators and the Mythic Imagination* (Amherst, NY)

Ward, Peter, and Joe Kirschvink, *A New History of Life: The Radical New Discoveries about the Origins and Evolution of Life on Earth* (New York, 2015)

Wendt, Herbert, *In Search of Adam: The Story of Man's Quest for the Truth about His Earliest Ancestors* (Boston, MA, 1956)

Wilford, John Noble, *The Riddle of the Dinosaurs* (New York, 1985)

Worster, Donald, *Nature's Economy: A History of Ecological Ideas* (Cambridge, 1994)

ACKNOWLEDGEMENTS

I thank my wife, Linda Sax, for reading over drafts of the chapters in this book and offering many valuable corrections and suggestions. I am also grateful to the team at Reaktion Books for their confidence in this work. This book has given me an opportunity to revisit parts of my childhood and think about all of the debts that are, inevitably, unmentioned and even unrecognized. A big 'thank you' to all!

PHOTO ACKNOWLEDGEMENTS

The author and the publishers wish to express their thanks to the below sources of illustrative material and/or permission to reproduce it:

Alamy: pp. 95 (Photo 12), 126 (Natural History Museum, London), 144 (Everett Collection Inc.); Scott Robert Anselmo: p. 99; taraBlazkova: p. 173; courtesy of Carl Buell: pp. 163 (top and bottom), 243; Alessio Damato: p. 110; Jerrye and Roy Klotz MD: p. 209 (top); Library of Congress, Washington, DC: pp. 40, 137, 184; Jud McCranie: p. 129; The Metropolitan Museum of Art, New York: p. 27 (Elisha Whittelsey Collection/The Elisha Whittelsey Fund, 1949); Tom Page: p. 114; REX Shutterstock: p. 213 bottom (Moviestore Collection); Nick Richards: p. 118 (top); Boria Sax: pp. 11, 178, 181, 209 (top), 224; Shutterstock: pp. 10 (Shujaa_777), 22 (Predrag Sepelj), 73 (Dziurek), 127 (alredosaz), 139 (Nor Gal), 170 (rook79), 188 (AustralianCamera), 213 top (Knot Mirai), 225 (AKKHARAT JARUSILAWONG), 242 (Suwat wongkham); Ian Wright: p. 118 (bottom).

INDEX